The Little Book

of

THE

CIVIL WAR

The Little Book
of
THE
CIVIL WAR

by

HARRY ADÈS

p

This is a Parragon Publishing Book
First published in 2001

Parragon Publishing
Queen Street House
4 Queen Street
Bath BA1 1HE, UK

Produced by Magpie Books, an imprint of
Constable & Robinson Publishing Ltd, London

Copyright © Parragon 2001

Cover illustration courtesy of Mary Evans Picture Library

ISBN 0-75255-918-4

A copy of the British Library Cataloguing-in-Publication Data
is available from the British Library
Printed in China

Contents

Introduction

No single event in the history of America has had such a profound effect on the nation as the Civil War. No event has been more costly to its people either. More soldiers lost their lives in this catastrophic episode than in all its other conflicts combined.

Today it is difficult to imagine how men in their hundreds of thousands could take arms against their friends and relatives, their neighbors and countrymen, and wage brutal, furious war. And yet, this is what happened just two lifetimes ago, for four bloody years between 1861 and 1865 – a savage convulsion that drew a deep line between the America before and the America after.

Why such passion and bitterness erupted into such violent and protracted conflict has long been a matter of intense debate. In the mid-nineteenth century, it seemed republics had a habit of ending in ruin, bloodshed, or despotism. The brave young

American Republic, however, strove to be different. It was a republic "conceived in liberty" by its founding fathers, but just how that liberty should best be expressed was not yet clear.

During the Civil War both sides were fighting for their own ideas of liberty. In the South it was for the freedom of individual states to choose their own political course. In the North it was for the indivisible Union, in which they believed lay the best chance for preserving the Republic, and the ideals of liberty and democracy that it embodied. And mixed into this argument was another explosive contradiction. How could a nation that declared all men are created equal and are equally entitled to "life, liberty, and the pursuit of happiness" also exploit four million slaves – and be the largest slave-owning country in the world? Such tangled questions had haunted the United States since its inception. In 1861, they could be left unanswered no longer.

By the time the Civil War drew to a close, after the heroes had been lauded and the leaders immortalized, after the battlefields had been cleared and the dead buried, the nation had stumbled upon an answer. It was an answer that defined today's

United States, that created a "new birth of freedom" for its people, and that helped secure America's place as the most powerful and influential nation on earth.

Chapter One

Unhappy Union

A house divided against itself cannot stand. I believe this government cannot endure, permanently half slave and half free.

Abraham Lincoln

A House Divided

Less than thirty years before the outbreak of the Civil War, Alexis de Tocqueville wrote that the American people was "one of the happiest in the world." Indeed, he had every reason to be impressed with the young Republic, a proud democracy steadily growing in confidence and prosperity, a nation further cemented by a shared language, religion, political and legal system, and culture. And yet, despite so much going for it, by the mid-nineteenth century the Union was in crisis – the North and South of the country were drifting irreconcilably apart.

The northern states had been enjoying the fruits of the early industrial age; cities were springing up as immigrants rushed in for work, and transportation links were improving apace to support the robust growth. Meanwhile the southern economy was far less dynamic, dominated as it was by agriculture, in particular huge cotton plantations that satisfied an enormous global demand for the crop. Southerners too had begun to resent federal policies which they believed benefited the North at their expense. And as they saw the North becoming more powerful, they feared that eventually their interests would be excluded altogether. Whispers of secession and a firm commitment to states' rights became increasingly important on the political landscape of the South.

Most historians, however, now agree that these differences between the sections were not enough alone to spark off the worst war in American history. Many think that the superficial rift between an industrial North and agricultural South would have been healed by political compromise. Crucially, the enmity between the two sections was greatly – and tragically – complicated by the South's dependence on slavery. In combination with all the other antagonisms, the growing rancor over slavery served to push the country over the brink into war. Though it was not the sole reason for the Civil War, many believe that the bloodshed would probably have been averted had slavery been abolished long before.

Slavery – The "Peculiar Institution"

By 1850, slavery had died out in the northern states, mainly because it was no longer profitable, but also due to the growing moral unease with the institution.

In stark contrast, four million slaves were the engine of the southern economy, providing indispensable labor not only in the fields, but in a wide range of occupations, from railroad workers to coal miners. Above all, it was the rise of the cotton plantations that ensured slavery flourished in the South. Thanks to the invention of the cotton gin by Eli Whitney in 1793 – a cheap and efficient machine that could separate the seeds from the fiber – cotton was suddenly the most profitable southern crop (far outstripping tobacco, rice, and sugar). With the exploitation of slave labor it could be cultivated in vast quantities at relatively little cost. On the eve of the war, slave labor enabled the South to harvest three-quarters of the world's cotton, worth almost $200 million – well over half the value of all America's exports.

As it happened, however, the majority of whites in the South were not actually slave owners. Around a quarter of all white households kept slaves, and more than half of these owned less than five slaves. In fact, only a tiny fraction of households – less than one percent – held estates with over a hundred slaves. Even so, the market value of the slaves was $3 billion – more than the worth of the land and the cotton put

Slave Cabin

together. With so much money at stake, it is not surprising that most white southern farmers who did not possess slaves not only supported slavery, but aspired to become slave-holders themselves. A slave was not simply viewed as cheap labor, but as a sound investment for the future. Farmers tried to encourage slaves to reproduce almost as they would livestock, knowing that a child could fetch $100 at market, and could grow into a fit young man worth as much as $2000.

But while the South grew rich on the back of slave labor, the North was becoming increasingly unhappy about such a degrading and cruel institution. By 1830, abolitionists were achieving prominence in

Slave Orderly

northern politics and were attracting a steadily burgeoning body of support. Within three decades, the debates over the issue were passionate. Most people believed the nation's two systems of slave labor and free labor were "incongruous", "incompatible," and "irreconcilable."

Unfortunately, the greater the northern attacks on slavery became, the more the South lurched to its defense. Southerners termed slavery as their "peculiar institution" – a special part of the southern way of life that distinguished them from the rest. Slavery was the bedrock of southern society, and as such most southerners held their peculiar institution in very high esteem. Indeed, many would be willing to fight and die to protect it.

The Abolition Movement

By the 1830s, the movement to abolish slavery could no longer be ignored. A growing body of activists loudly condemned the institution as a gross violation of the ideals of liberty upon which America was built. Among them was William Lloyd Garrison, perhaps the most persistent and passionate in his attacks. In 1831, at the age of twenty-five, Garrison founded *The Liberator*, a journal devoted to the abolitionist cause. His words in his first editorial signaled his fervor: "I am in earnest – I will not equivocate – I will not excuse – I will not retreat a single inch – and *I will be heard.*"

Working with only one helper for twelve hours a day, Garrison's message was indeed heard – even if his paper never made a profit. In just a few years, his call for the immediate and unconditional end to slavery had aroused the emotions of the public to such an extent that at times his own safety was in question. Once he was forced to take refuge in a Boston jail, when white laborers went on the rampage, protesting that their jobs would be at risk from freed slaves.

The anti-slavery movement won further encouragement in 1833, when the British Parliament resolved to abolish slavery throughout the Empire. As a result, the New York reformers Arthur and Lewis Tappan founded the American Anti-Slavery Society with sixty-one other abolitionists who rallied behind the common belief that humans could not be chattels like "brute beasts," especially not in a country whose venerated Declaration of Independence held that "all men are created equal." Combining abolitionism with a religious zeal, agents were sent out armed with sheaves of pamphlets, preaching against the great sin of slavery to recruit members. A deluge of anti-slavery literature rained down upon the general public – in one year alone, the Society printed almost 650,000 fliers, tracts, and papers – in an unstinting effort to educate against the evils of the peculiar institution. Their hard work was spectacularly successful, and in five years more than 1300

Frederick Douglass

abolitionist societies had been founded in the North, with a total membership of around a quarter of a million people.

A member of one such society was Frederick Douglass, one of the most eloquent speakers against slavery in America. As a runaway slave himself, Douglass could speak with the authenticity that white campaigners could never have, describing the cruelty and degradation of slavery with the clarity of firsthand experience. Never afraid to speak his mind, Douglass often lambasted his white audiences, shocking and shaming them into action and commitment to the movement. At one speech he told a rapt crowd that slavery's existence "brands your republicanism as a sham, your humanity as a base pretense, your Christianity as a lie." At others he would begin, "I appear this evening as a thief and robber. I stole this head, these limbs, this body from my master, and ran off with them." His wit and honesty quickly won many sympathizers and challenged the racial prejudices of even those whites who claimed to be anti-slavery. Douglass saw that beyond the slavery issue was one of racial justice and equality. Black people needed the same rights as their white counterparts, they should be able to enjoy the same transport facilities, education services, and right to vote. As it was, black people were not even allowed to testify against whites in court.

With money given to him by a wide circle of friends and admirers, Douglass was able to buy his freedom, and set up his own influential journal, the *North Star*, later known as *Frederick Douglass' Paper*.

Opposition to Change

In 1831, eight months after William Lloyd Garrison had launched *The Liberator*, the slave Nat Turner led a violent slave rebellion in Virginia which resulted in

Slave and Child

the deaths of fifty-seven whites, and inflamed southern sentiments against the abolitionists. The rebel slaves were mercilessly hunted down, many of them being killed without trial, others being tried and executed. Vigilante bands roamed the country exacting brutal retribution on any black people that they came across. It is estimated that hundreds of innocent people were murdered in the backlash. Some southern states even offered a $5000 reward for Garrison's capture, and Louisiana put a colossal $50,000 price tag on Arthur Tappan, founder of the American Anti-Slavery Society.

The flood of "incendiary" literature pouring into the South from northern printing presses also alarmed the slave-holders. Southern states passed laws so that anti-slavery material could be seized on arrival. In some cases, the whip was meted out to black people that sought out the forbidden literature. Congress even put itself under the so-called "gag rule" which held that petitions on slavery should not be debated in the House. The rule stood for almost a decade before it fell in 1845.

By far the worst obstacle that the abolitionists had to face was mob violence targeted against them. Hundreds of riots erupted at anti-slavery lectures and demonstrations, often headed by community leaders, prominent professionals, and local businessmen. Speakers were pelted with stones and rotten fruit, while agitators heckled and shouted to drown out their words. The abolitionist cause gained its first martyr in 1837, the anti-slavery publisher, Elijah Lovejoy, who was forced to move his printing operation from Missouri to Alton, Illinois, where he had it under armed guard. A mob finally hurled his press into the Ohio River and shot him five times.

The extremes that the rioters were willing to go to

was indication of their intense fear of abolition. Slave insurrections such as Nat Turner's sent waves of panic through the South; angry slaves once freed, they thought, would only seek violent revenge on their masters. As slaves, the black population was controlled and suppressed. Abolition also meant the end of a labor system that was the cornerstone of southern life.

The North also harbored strong anti-abolitionist sentiment, in most part based on the profound racial prejudices prevalent at the time. For some northerners, the anti-slavery group represented something un-American and even anarchic. They thought the abolitionists menaced traditional forms of authority and the fragile sense of nation that had recently taken root. By loudly applauding the British abolition of slavery as something more important than the triumph of the American Revolution, by touring the country with British abolitionists, by appealing to women and people of color – two disenfranchised groups – and by lecturing alongside black people in the name of racial equality, the abolitionists were in many people's eyes subversive agitators determined to turn the conventional order of things to chaos.

Ironically, the success of pro-slavery activism ended up playing an important part in slavery's ultimate downfall. As powerful anti-abolitionists shut off avenues of expression in the press and in politics, as they limited the circulation of abolitionist literature, intimidated speakers and stifled political debate, the mood of northern pro-slavery sympathizers began to shift. The principles of free speech as enshrined in the Bill of Rights were being whittled down by the pro-slavers, and abolitionists conversely become the guardians of the great ideals of American liberty and freedom of expression. For many northerners, the abolitionists' image as subversives faded away, and the perceived danger of their anti-slavery position started to be outweighed by the desire to see free speech defended and liberty upheld.

The Missouri Compromise

The slavery issue gripped the American consciousness in the mid-nineteenth century like at no other time, but the whole debate had been simmering away right from the very inception of the American nation. The Founding Fathers correctly recognized the danger that disagreement over slavery held for the young Union, and chose to exclude the whole troublesome matter from the political forum by denying Congress the authority to regulate slavery.

But it was a problem that would not stay in the shadows for long. In 1819, slavery burst back onto the political stage when Missouri was about to form a constitution with a view to becoming a state. An amendment was tabled effectively ensuring that it would not be a slave-holding state. Party lines collapsed as Representatives regrouped according to whether they were from the North or the South. The northerners narrowly won the vote, but a deadlock was reached after the Senate blocked the amendment, until a solution, known as the Missouri Compromise, was agreed the following year. The new state was admitted to the Union as slave-holding, but with the condition that no other slave states should be allowed north of the parallel that made Missouri's southern boundary. For the time being, it seemed this might put the problem to bed, but ex-President John Quincy Adams was more far-sighted, calling the Compromise "a title page to a great, tragic volume."

War with Mexico

As we have seen, the slavery issue was bubbling away during the 1830s, but it boiled over once again after the War with Mexico of 1846. The President, James K. Polk of Tennessee, with the help of his generals Zachary Taylor and Winfield Scott – both southerners – gained an enormous new territory from Mexico encompassing the present-day states of Utah, Nevada, Arizona, and California, and parts of Colorado, New Mexico, and Wyoming.

As soon as the land was won, the debate raged whether it should be slave or free. The South saw this as its great chance to expand slavery westward, an opportunity that could only better its economic and political power. Texas was already overrun with slave-holding settlers and was accepted into the Union as a slave state. The rest of the new territory, on the other hand, did not have slaves, and both sections launched into bitter argument about what should be done with it.

In addition to the pro- and anti-slavery contingents from South and North, other groups sought more moderate, halfway solutions, such as extending the line of the Missouri Compromise all the way to the Pacific. Others wanted the matter to be decided by "popular sovereignty" – in other words, allow settlers to move in whether they owned slaves or not, and let them decide if the state should be free when it was time for it to join the Union.

The nation began to sink into a political quagmire as parties disintegrated and reformed along sectional lines. As the election of 1848 approached, the main anti-slavery groups convened at Buffalo and formed a third party, the Free-Soil party, which adhered to the Wilmot Proviso – legislation banning slavery from any part of the new territory. The Free-Soilers fought a brave campaign, but receiving ten percent of the vote, could not beat

Senator William Seward

the honed organizations of the Democratic and Whig party machines. Though defeated, the Free-Soilers forced the two major parties to appeal to anti-slavery feeling in defense of their vote, effectively making the whole issue a central and, according to Senator William Seward, "respectable element" in American politics.

The Compromise of 1850

When gold was struck in the Sacramento Valley, California in January 1848, the headlong rush of prospectors precipitated an immediate crisis. Around 80,000 "Forty-Niners," as they were known, surged into the territory seeking their fortune. A decision had to be made quickly about California's status, but Washington was still in the grip of sectional turmoil and murmurs of southern secession echoed around Capitol Hill.

Henry Clay, a long-serving Representative and Senator who had previously engineered the Missouri Compromise, was called upon once again. His solution – the Compromise of 1850 – was delicately balanced. Amongst other measures, it stipulated that California was to be admitted as a free state; the territories of New Mexico and Utah were to be set up without mention of slavery (the decision would be up to future settlers); the slave trade would be outlawed in the District of Columbia; and laws regarding the capture and return of escaped slaves be tightened.

As ever with a compromise, none of the factions was completely happy, but as it was widely believed to be the only way out the problem, it was passed through Congress. For the moment, at least, the slavery problem seemed to have been settled.

The Fugitive Slave Act

The optimism, however, was short-lived. For northerners, the Fugitive Slave Act was the most disagreeable part of the compromise, and dozens of communities would not enforce it. The law imposed large fines on anyone who helped slaves to freedom or refused to detain escaped slaves. Furthermore, captured fugitives were to be refused the right of trial by jury. In the end, such draconian measures only exacerbated northern antipathy toward the South, and aroused greater anti-slavery sentiment in some people than all the abolitionists' politicking of previous decades.

Ironically, the Underground Railroad – a network of safe-houses and sympathizers who helped slaves escape to the free North and, better still, Canada – flourished in direct contravention of the new laws. The system was informal, secretive, and without leader, but had established itself all across the North in spite of the penalties. Upward of 40,000 slaves were spirited away to freedom during the Railroad's existence.

The animosity awakened by the fugitive laws also spawned one of the most devastating pieces of anti-slavery propaganda to capture the American people's imagination. Stung into action by laws she regarded "a nightmare abomination," Harriet Beecher Stowe wrote *Uncle Tom's Cabin*, a melodramatic story about the unhappy life of Tom, a gentle Kentucky slave, and his abysmal treatment by his masters. In its first year, the novel sold well over a million copies in the United States and England, and was soon translated into dozens of languages. By today's standards, the novel's characters seem two-dimensional and stereotyped, but at the time the book was hailed as a masterpiece, winning Stowe praise from Leo Tolstoy

Harriet Beecher Stowe

and Heinrich Heine, and audiences with Charles Dickens and Queen Victoria. More importantly, it strongly appealed to popular feeling in the North and united opinion behind the anti-slavery cause more effectively than anything had before it.

The Kansas-Nebraska Act

Just as anti-slavery feeling was intensifying in the North, so was resentment in the South. To upset matters even further, Senator Stephen A. Douglas of Illinois introduced the ill-fated Kansas-Nebraska Act, which only pushed the country a step closer to war. He proposed the creation of two new territories, Kansas and Nebraska, the people of which would presently decide whether they would be slave-holding or free. Amid turbulent debate, the Act was passed by the Senate in May 1854, thus nullifying the provisions of the Missouri Compromise and destroying whatever fragile agreement there was between sections.

Thousands of highly politicized, and often armed, settlers from both sides came to settle Kansas, determined to take it for the cause of freedom or slavery. Tempers ran at fever pitch and the stage was set for bloodshed. Raids, torchings, looting, and shootings between free-soil and pro-slavery settlers tore the territory in two. Guerrilla bands and militiamen presided over the anarchy as the rival groups hurried to form their own legislatures.

The violence even spilled over into the Senate.

Senator Sumner of Massachusetts had delivered a withering tirade about the "crime against Kansas", attacking South Carolina's Senator Butler amongst others. Sumner was bludgeoned with a cane to the point of death on the Senate floor by Butler's nephew.

The Dred Scott Case

To confuse matters further, the Supreme Court – supposedly removed from the intractable conflict of partisan politics – stepped into the fray with a highly controversial decision. Dred Scott was a Missouri slave whose master was posted as army surgeon for four years in Illinois and Wisconsin Territory. When his master died, Scott sued for freedom on the grounds that he had spent four years in areas where slavery had been outlawed. The case worked its way up to the Supreme Court, where its southern majority ruled that Scott had no right to sue at all as, being a slave, he was not a citizen of the United States. Moreover, the Court claimed that residence in a free state did not automatically make a slave free, as Congress was not entitled to remove property from a citizen without the appropriate backing of the legal system. The ruling meant that the Missouri Compromise had been unconstitutional, and by implication Congress did not have the power to keep slavery from the territories.

In practical terms, the ruling actually had little real effect. It did, however, greatly deepen the hostility and wariness between North and South.

The Republican Party

In all the political confusion and sectional strife brought about by the Kansas-Nebraska Act, the Whig party disintegrated. Its anti-slavery remnants joined forces with the Free-Soil party and a number of smaller groups who sought the limitation of slavery in the West and the economic advancement of the industrial North.

The new party held its first convention in 1856 in Philadelphia and chose John Frémont as its first presidential candidate. In the elections of that year, the Republicans took control of large swathes of the North, but had virtually no support in the South and could not clinch the presidency from the Democratic nominee, James Buchanan.

It was widely predicted that the Republicans could only improve their vote in the next election, and prominent party members, such as William Seward and Salmon P. Chase, began jostling for position to be presidential nominee.

Abraham Lincoln

A gawky Illinois lawyer was also making a name for himself within the Republican party. Abraham Lincoln's shrewd mind, honest character, and amiable disposition had brought him from humble beginnings to threshold of political success.

Born in a log cabin in Kentucky in 1809, Lincoln grew up with a largely illiterate family that scraped its meager living from the wilderness. From an early age, he showed a keen wit and soon learnt to read even though he had had less than a year of formal education. His father could barely scrawl his own name. At twenty-two Lincoln settled in New Salem, Illinois, eager to broaden his horizons. Here he flung himself into a number of jobs — store owner, postmaster, rail-splitter, surveyor, even operator of a whiskey still. In his six years at New Salem he had

Abraham Lincoln

also learnt much about the vicissitudes of life, from falling in love to being declared bankrupt, from fighting Black Hawk as a captain in a militia to mastering the law. It was in New Salem too, that Lincoln had his first taste of politics and when he left the town to go to Springfield, the new state capital, it was as a State legislator.

In Springfield, he built a reputation as an accomplished lawyer and married Mary Ann Todd, who came from a well-to-do slave-owning family from Lexington, Kentucky. Before long, he had established himself as a promising politician and an accomplished lawyer, with a gift for home-spun rhetoric that could charm and win over a crowd.

Although not an out-and-out abolitionist (he believed slavery could not be constitutionally outlawed), Lincoln had seized the slavery issue with alacrity and argued forcefully that it was morally wrong and as such should be restricted in a way that would ensure its "ultimate extinction." Succumbing to the prejudices of the time, however, Lincoln did not believe in total racial equality and maintained that whites held a "superior position." But he did firmly believe that the Declaration of Independence applied to all humans, and that black people were fully entitled to the rights guaranteed by it. The Republicans still harbored a range of views on slavery, but Lincoln skillfully united extremists and moderates behind him.

The Lincoln-Douglas Debates

Lincoln's great chance to shine came in 1858, when he challenged Democratic Senator Douglas, the instigator of the Kansas-Nebraska controversy, for the Illinois seat in the US Senate. Douglas was nicknamed the "Little Giant," a diminutive man in stature at five foot four with a towering reputation as an orator. A series of seven debates were organized around Illinois with slavery as the main topic for discussion. Suave, flashy, short, and plump, Douglas appeared the perfect opposite to Lincoln, who stood awkward and thin at six foot four, often in ill-fitting clothes. As speakers, however, they were a fine match and their debates caught the attention of the whole country.

Lincoln began with the now immortal "House Divided" speech, in which he warned that the Union would collapse if it remained "half-slave and half-free." Lincoln forced Douglas to spell out his "popular sovereignty" point of view, which held that slavery could be abolished in the new territories if settlers wanted it, regardless of the Dred Scott decision – a view which cost Douglas many southern votes two years later, and drove a wedge through the Democratic party.

Douglas went on to win the Senate election, but Lincoln was the real winner. He had shot from relative obscurity to national fame; and his performances all but secured him his nomination as Republican presidential candidate.

John Brown

In October 1859, at a time when sectional discord was already at crisis level, John Brown, a hardened anti-slavery extremist, planned a daring raid on the Federal arsenal at Harper's Ferry in Virginia. His idea was to use the arms to spark off a slave uprising, which he hoped would quickly escalate into widespread rebellion. Three years earlier, Brown had already achieved notoriety in Kansas when he and his band murdered five slave-holding settlers at Pottawatomie Creek. To radicals, however, he was a hero.

At nightfall, Brown and his men took control of

John Brown

Harper's Ferry

the town's armory, arsenal, and engine house, and rounded up hostages. From then on, his harebrained scheme went sour. The town's station baggage master, Shephard Hayward, was shot by Brown's men; he was the first to fall, and a free black man. When the alarm was raised, the local militia drove Brown into the engine house. Shortly afterward, the marines under a Colonel Robert E. Lee arrived and stormed in, taking Brown prisoner and killing six of his seventeen men, including two of his sons. A week later Brown was charged with insurrection, treason, and murder, and after a swift trial, was found guilty on all counts. On December 2, 1859, he was hanged.

To southerners, he personified everything to be feared and hated in abolitionism: aggression, violence, and the will to incite slaves to bloody revolution. If this is what the abolitionists wanted, they believed, then no southern state was safe. In the eyes of many northerners, on the other hand, Brown was a martyr who had laid down his life to rid the land of slavery. His name would even be immortalized in song to the tune of Battle Hymn of the Republic.

After the Brown raid, a peaceful end to the sectional strife seemed virtually impossible. Violence hung in the air and the sense of emergency deepened as the nation prepared itself for the 1860 presidential elections.

Chapter Two

The Call to Arms

This Southern Confederacy must be supported now by calm determination and cool brains. We have risked all and we must play our best, for the stake is life or death.

Mary Chesnut

The Sixteenth President

Following Abraham Lincoln's success and popularity on the platform in the Douglas debates, it seemed he was the natural choice for the Republican party's presidential candidate. The Democrats were a split party and ended up fielding two nominees; Douglas was chosen to represent northern Democratic interests, and John C. Breckinridge the southern wing. Disaffected Whigs from the border states formed the Constitutional Union Party and backed John C. Bell of Tennessee.

On the night of the 1860 election, it soon became clear that Lincoln had smashed his opponents in the

Abraham Lincoln

John C. Breckinridge

North. It turned out that he had just clinched the popular vote, but winning all eighteen free states, he had an easy majority in the electoral college. Breckinridge took all but four of the slave states, while Douglas came behind Lincoln in the popular vote, but only gained Missouri.

The result was clear: Abraham Lincoln was to be the first ever Republican President of the United States.

As soon as the result was in, however, there was trouble. The Republican election platform which included free territory and railroad subsidies summed up the political and economic interests of the North – interests that were anathema to the South. Few southerners wanted anything to do with the new administration. The Union itself was under threat.

Secession

The southern states feared nothing more than the Republicans winning the presidency. When their nightmares became reality, the response was swift and extreme. In December, the legislature of South Carolina set the ball rolling by calling a special state

Secession Rosette and Badge

Jefferson Davis

convention, which voted unanimously that the state should secede from the Union.

By February, Texas, Louisiana, Mississippi, Alabama, Georgia, and Florida had followed suit. Delegates from each state met in Montgomery, Alabama and drafted a new constitution for a new nation, the Confederate States of America. Jefferson Davis of Mississippi was chosen as the provisional President. He took his oath of office on February 18, 1861 on the steps of the new nation's capitol at Montgomery amid a crowd of happy southerners. "Upon my . . . head were showered smiles, plaudits, and flowers," Davis recalled, "but beyond them I saw troubles innumerable."

State House at Montgomery, Alabama

The act of secession was greeted across the deep South states with defiant elation. One Georgia newspaper said, "Whether the Potomac is crimsoned in human gore, and Pennsylvania Avenue is paved ten fathoms deep with mangled bodies . . . the South will never submit to such humiliation and degradation as the inauguration of Abraham Lincoln." A flurry of poems and songs were written in celebration.

In the North the atmosphere was very different. Congress scrabbled around desperately trying to find a way out of crisis; many in Washington still believed the seceded states would rejoin the Union as quickly as they had left, if the terms were right. Senator John J. Crittenden of Kentucky came up with a possible solution: the old Missouri Compromise line would be put back into effect, while the new territories could join the Union as slave or free through popular sovereignty; the fugitive slave laws would be more rigorously followed and government would be required to compensate slave owners with missing slaves; no amendments would be possible to the Constitution to afford Congress authority over slavery in any state.

President-elect Lincoln rejected the Crittenden Compromise. Having fought his campaign so firmly on limiting the spread of slavery, he could hardly agree to a course of action that would almost certainly contribute to its extension. With the Compromise in tatters, Lincoln's task of keeping the Union together was made even more difficult.

For the Sake of the Union

Less than three weeks after Jefferson Davis was sworn in, Abraham Lincoln took his presidential oaths in Washington on the steps of the unfinished Capitol. His inaugural address made it clear that he had no intention of letting the Union break up, something

Lincoln's Inauguration, 1861

with which most northerners wholeheartedly agreed.
To them, the Union was the world's greatest
experiment in republican self-government, and
secession would irrevocably weaken it. One
newspaper editor summed up the feeling aptly: "If the
minority have the right to break up the Government
at pleasure, because they have not had their way, there
is an end of all government." Quite apart from this,
northerners regarded secession as illegal. After all, it
was their view that the American people as a whole
had created the Union, and it was they as a whole who
owned the Union. Therefore it was the decision of all
the American people whether or not it should be
dismembered.

For Lincoln this was the root of the dispute between North and South over and above even the slavery issue. As President, he felt it was his constitutional duty to save the Union at any cost.

Fort Sumter

When the Southern states seceded, most of the Federal military installations in the South slipped into Confederate hands. In Lincoln's inaugural address, he said he would do everything possible to "hold, occupy, and possess" such places. None of them was more symbolic to the two sides than Fort Sumter, a squat, brick, island stronghold guarding Charleston Harbor, which remained in Union hands. The commanding officer, Major Robert Anderson, holed up in what was now effectively enemy territory, resolutely flew the United States flag above the fortress. To the people of

Fort Sumter

The First Shots

Charleston, the sight of it was a gross affront, and an insult to the new Confederate nation.

South Carolinians leaned heavily on Washington to have it peaceably evacuated, and deployed troops around the harbor to stop provisions reaching the fort. Lincoln had already committed himself to defend it and was not going to give it up easily. He sent a shipment of supplies, showing that he intended there to be a siege if necessary. As it happened, his actions went to little effect. Around midnight on April 12, an ultimatum from the Confederates was delivered to the fort giving the Federals four hours to surrender. Anderson refused to comply.

Fort Sumter in Rebel Hands

And so it was that, at 4.30am on April 12, 1861, the first shots of the American Civil War were fired. The South Carolina batteries opened up, shelling the beleaguered fort for thirty-four hours until Major Anderson finally lowered the flag over and surrendered. Ironically, America's bloodiest war began without a single fatality.

Lincoln knew he was bound to lose the fort, but more importantly for him, the Confederates had been the aggressors, and the burden of war lay on their shoulders. News of the assault would only outrage the North and help unify northern opinion against the South.

Union Regulars, 1861

Enlistment

In early 1861, the United States' diminutive army consisted of 16,000 regulars mostly positioned on outposts in the West to deal with sporadic Indian uprisings. Many of the officers and most experienced soldiers resigned after the attack of Fort Sumter to side with the South. What was left to the Union was clearly woefully inadequate to fight a war. The top-ranking army chiefs were almost all veterans of the Anglo-American War of 1812 – as old as the vintage flintlock muskets which took up a large proportion of the Federal arsenals.

8th NY Volunteers

Within a couple of days of losing Fort Sumter, Lincoln called on the Union states to summon up 75,000 ninety-day volunteers to help stamp order on the country and quell the "insurrection," and a further 42,000 to enlist for three years' service. The response across the North was boundlessly enthusiastic. In Ohio, for example, where thirteen regiments had been called for, men rushed to joined up, swelling the ranks of twenty regiments.

The southern Union states, however, were far more ambivalent. They had been put on the spot by Lincoln's call to arms, and now had to commit themselves to one side or the other. The hope that the rift between sections might be healed was dead and a

Jefferson Davis's Residence in Richmond

decision now had to be made. On April 17, Virginia voted for secession, and North Carolina, Arkansas, and Tennessee followed a few weeks later. Jefferson Davis was delighted that Virginia had joined the Confederacy – it was the most heavily populated and industrialized slave state – and promptly moved the capital from Montgomery to Richmond in appreciation. Now the enemy capitals stood just eighty miles apart "like queens at chess upon adjacent squares" as Winston Churchill imagined.

The drive to enlist in the South was no less eager. Some 20,000 men – about a third of those who tried to join up – had to be sent home because quotas were already full. On both sides, men wanted a piece

New Confederate Recruits

of the action, and many thought the war would be over in a matter of weeks. Some even worried that the fighting would end before they had a chance to taste the "fun."

A Fair Match?

As the two sides squared up for war, it seemed clear that the North had an overwhelming material advantage. In numbers alone, the twenty three states of the Union contained a population of 22 million people, against the 9 million of the eleven Confederate states – almost 4 million of whom were slaves and prohibited from fighting. In terms of infrastructure too, the South lagged far behind; of

30,000 miles of railroad track laid just nine thousand miles serviced Confederate territory. Likewise with industry and raw materials, such as copper, iron, and coal, the North had a huge lead over the South.

But a war is not waged on wealth and resources alone. Morale, attitude, and experience can also be vitally important. It was generally accepted that the southern states bred the most accomplished soldiers. Indeed, many of the old Union army's highest ranks were taken by southerners. Many of the greatest, including Robert E. Lee and Thomas J. "Stonewall" Jackson left the Union army before the outset of war to join the Confederates.

The farming life of the South was also recognized as a fine training ground for skills used in battle. On

Confederate Horseman

the southern farms and plantations children grew up learning how to shoot and ride. As one Charleston newspaper boasted, "Our raw troops are far superior to the raw troops of the United States. Our people are used to arms. They are accustomed to the gun and the horse. The people of the North can neither shoot a rifle nor ride a horse, unless trained." The *Raleigh Banner* was even more graphic: "The army of the South will be composed of the best material that ever yet made up an army; while that of Lincoln will be gathered from the sewers of the cities – the degraded, beastly offscourings of all the quarters of the world, who will serve for pay and will run away as soon as they can when danger threatens."

Southerners thought they had another card up their sleeve. Cotton may not be the most important natural resource in warfare, but having a huge share of the world market was bound to secure influence overseas. The mills of Britain and France, for instance, and the livelihoods of hundreds of thousands of people depended on southern cotton. It was thought that the European powers might intervene to protect the cotton trade, perhaps recognizing the Confederacy as a nation, perhaps trying to bring the war to an early close.

Moreover, the war would be fought in the South; all it had to do was to successfully defend to win. The pressure was on the North to invade – it could only be victorious if it destroyed the "rogue" government, finish the Confederacy and return the seceded states to the Union. This task was clearly much harder to achieve than to prevent, and was to go a long way in leveling the balance of power. The North was going to need every advantage available to it.

The Border States

With such a delicate balance of power, it was absolutely critical that Lincoln kept the border states, Kentucky, Missouri, Delaware, and Maryland, in the Union. These were slave states that had not yet seceded, since popular opinion on the slavery issue was split about down the middle in each. If they were to defect to the Confederacy, then the Union's task would very much more difficult.

Kentucky found itself with a Unionist legislature and a secessionist governor, and fearing the worst kind of internecine violence, declared itself neutral. It suited both Davis and Lincoln to leave it that way for the present; any interference was likely to push the state into their opponents' hands.

Maryland and Missouri were more volatile and required a firmer hand. Just after Fort Sumter, the 6th Massachusetts Regiment found itself marching through Baltimore on its way to defend Washington. A strong pro-southern sentiment was prevalent in Baltimore, and before long the regiment found that it had attracted unwanted attention. Jeering and name-calling soon degenerated into scuffles as fights broke out, and inevitably the soldiers resorted to turning their guns on the mob. Thirteen people were killed, including nine civilians. When Lincoln heard, he sent forces to occupy Baltimore and threw secessionist members of the legislature in jail until

6th Massachusetts Regiment

the Unionist governor could gain total control — hard-arm tactics that ensured the state would stay in the Union.

In Missouri, the pro-Confederate governor had provocatively placed a body of state troops just outside St. Louis, ominously close to a Federal arsenal there. Unionists feared that the governor had designs on it, and worse, could use the arms to force Missouri into the Confederacy. Captain Nathaniel S. Lyon was sent to break up the encampment and save 21,000 muskets from southern hands, which he did efficiently and peacefully. As he marched back to barracks with his men, a mob gathered and started to pelt them with stones. In the fracas a captain was shot. Lyon's troops retaliated, firing volleys into the crowd and killing twenty-eight people.

Lyon was a young and ambitious hothead, and took it upon himself to drive all armed Confederates from the state. He ventured into south-western Missouri, a rebel stronghold and in a sharp engagement at Wilson's Creek he was killed. His troops retreated and the pro-southern elements regained control of that whole region. Meanwhile, his impetuous actions had aroused much ill-feeling in the divided state, an antipathy that fast descended into a vicious guerrilla war. It lasted for the next four years, but the animosities and sense of aggrievement would take decades to wear away.

Tense Preparation

High spirits and over-confidence on both sides fostered the popular belief that the war would be short and glorious. A couple of decisive battles would fix the matter once and for all. Few of the leaders, Lincoln included, were as optimistic, though they probably would not have anticipated the protracted destruction that the Civil War would bring.

The more experienced generals recognized that it

General Winfield Scott

would take time to assemble supplies and train the large number of new recruits. General-in-Chief Winfield Scott, a seventy-four-year-old veteran of the War of 1812 who suffered from dropsy and vertigo, devised a plan of methodical preparation. He held raw volunteer troops in low esteem and considered the ninety-day recruits as little better than worthless. Time would be needed to train the men up, establish supply lines, and produce all the armaments, clothing and equipment that should be in abundance before the war really got underway.

The South was in an even worse state of preparation. Federal arsenals before secession held around half a million weapons, and only about 135,000 of them were in the southern states. Even worse, just 10,000 of these seized arms were modern rifles, the rest being outdated smoothbores and flintlocks. Had the South used its huge stocks of cotton to trade for arms and ammunition with the European powers, they could have corrected their serious deficiency early on. Instead they opted for a policy of cutting their exports to the Old World, with the aim of forcing Britain and France, countries with major cotton-based industries, to intervene in the war and recognize the Confederacy as a legitimate

A Union Battery

nation. The calculation had not, however, reckoned on the fact that Britain and France had plenty of cotton thanks to a bumper crop the year before, and would not be under any pressure to intervene for months to come.

Plans for Attack

General Scott's offensive strategy was careful and considered. He wanted to enforce a blockade on the South at sea and along the Mississippi to starve the under-resourced section of essential supplies while the Union trained its troops. He expected this to bring the rebel government down "with less bloodshed than any other plan." As it turned out, his idea contained the seed of future Union victory, but in the euphoric moments of early 1861 the public clamored for a demonstrative exhibition of northern power. They wanted to teach the "impudent" Confederates a short, sharp lesson, namely by destroying the rebel army at one fell swoop.

The northern press rounded on Scott, deriding his idea to slowly strangle the South as the "Anaconda Plan." The most vociferous detractor was Horace Greeley, the influential Republican editor of the New York *Tribune*, who demanded that the Union march on Richmond posthaste. "Forward to Richmond!" Greeley's headline shouted. "Forward to Richmond! The Rebel Congress must Not be Allowed to Meet There on the 20th of July. By that date the place must be held by the National Army."

By the summer of 1861, 35,000 volunteer troops had convened on Washington, led by General Irvin McDowell. Most northerners – volunteer recruits included – were anxious to get the fighting started. Lincoln too was keen to make the most of the ninety-day volunteers, whose contracts would soon be at an

end. McDowell, on the other hand, was reluctant and shared General Scott's view that his troops were too raw to be effective. He wrote to Lincoln of his fears: "This is not an army. It will take a long time to make an army." The President's reply was cajoling: "You are green, it is true, but they are green, also; you are all green alike."

Twenty thousand soldiers of the Confederate army under General Pierre G. T. Beauregard, the debonair leader who had taken Fort Sumter a few months earlier, had meantime gathered at Manassas Junction, by the river of Bull Run, just twenty-five miles south-west of Washington. It was an important strategic location which commanded the Manassas Gap Railroad west to the Shenandoah Valley. The Confederates desperately wanted to control this railroad, which would allow them to move their

General Pierre G. T. Beauregard

relatively scant forces from one side of the Blue Ridge to the other quickly.

Lincoln and his generals also saw the importance of Manassas and they resolved that McDowell was to advance on it, while General Robert Patterson and his 16,000 troops would move to Harper's Ferry at the northern end of the Shenandoah and engage Joseph Johnston's army of around 9000, preventing them from supplying reinforcements at Manassas. On July 16, McDowell and his men set out for Manassas, a long and ill-disciplined line who commonly broke rank to pick blackberries and fetch water. In the heat of mid-July they marched slowly with their fifty-pound packs, and it took them almost

Confederate Fortifications near Manassas Junction

three days to cover the twenty-five miles, a distance that would take a trained corps under a day.

Unknown to McDowell, Beauregard had plenty of warning of the Union's arrival. In addition to Confederate intelligence in Washington, it seemed that most civilians in the capital had come out to watch the fighting, bringing their parasols and picnic hampers as on a summer outing. Beauregard readied his troops, ordering them to take up positions defending bridges and fords along eight miles of the Bull Run river, a couple of miles from Manassas Junction. Meanwhile in the east, Johnston outwitted the elderly Patterson, leaving him behind at Harper's

Ferry and out of the battle. By the time the fighting was under way, Johnston's men were swelling Confederate numbers, equaling those of the invaders.

First Manassas/Bull Run

Early in the morning of July 21, McDowell sent a column of 10,000 over the Bull Run two miles upriver of the Confederate line. Other regiments under General Tyler were sent to make a feint at one of the major – and heavily guarded – bridges on the river. The rebel commander at the bridge, the hard-drinking Colonel Nathan "Shanks" Evans, who had a servant on hand at all times with a large keg of whisky, quickly recognized the feint and maneuvered his forces north to meet the incoming Yankees.

Although hugely outnumbered, Evans rushed to the high ground at Matthews' Hill and kept the Union column pinned down for several hours, giving Beauregard vital time to reorganize his men and send new brigades to his left flank to make a new line. Eventually the greater Union strength started to show, and the rebels were forced back up the slopes of Henry House Hill. Mood in the northern camp was ecstatic; the civilians that had come to watch from Washington could taste Confederate defeat and waved their handkerchiefs with delight. McDowell also thought that it was over, and rode up to his men to congratulate them on winning a "great victory."

Just when all looked lost, a defining moment turned the tide of the battle. Rebel General Barnard Bee was attempting to pep up his demoralized troops and looking back at the hill cried, "There is Jackson standing like a stone wall." Whether or not this comment was inspirational or not – some have said that it was a point of criticism because Jackson and his men were stock still and not fighting at that time – the phrase came to immortalize one of the great generals of the Civil War. Bee and most of his regiment were killed shortly afterward, but Brigadier General Thomas J. Jackson and his men held firm and stopped the advancement of Federal forces. Jackson had earned his famous nickname "Stonewall."

As Federal guns and infantry supports stuttered on Henry House Hill, James E. B. ("Jeb") Stuart and his cavalry burst out of a wooded thicket onto the exposed Union flank. Seeing his chance, Stuart ordered a charge forcing the bulk of the Yankee army back. To

General Thomas J. "Stonewall" Jackson

confuse matters further a line of bluecoats began to advance on Federal forces from the top of the hill. Union commanders thought it might be some of their reinforcements, but the matter was settled when the advancing men — Jackson's 33rd Virginia — fired a volley, putting that part of the Federal line into total disarray. Having no standardized uniforms, and two very similar flags, mix-ups of identification were common that day. After the battle, Federal regiments took on blue uniforms and Confederates gray ones. General Beauregard designed the now familiar Confederate flag.

The balance of the battle was now swinging toward the Confederates as attack and counter attack raged across the hill. In the middle of it all, Henry House,

Confederate Flag

named after Judith Henry, an elderly, bedridden widow, was torn apart by shell fire, killing its occupant.

Late in the afternoon, Beauregard gave orders for an all-out attack; he could sense that Union resolve was faltering. Indeed, many of McDowell's men had been active since 2 a.m. that morning, without rest, food, and water. As the Confederates charged, Jackson told his men to scream. The rebel yell, as it became known, would strike terror into Union soldiers on many Civil War battlefields. "There is nothing like it on this side of the infernal region," one Union soldier recounted in the post-war years. "The peculiar corkscrew sensation that it sends down your backbone under these circumstances can never be told. You have to feel it, and if you say you did not feel it, and heard the yell, you have never been there."

Triumphant Rebels Advance

Exhausted, demoralized, and confused, the Federal brigades began to retreat. As the Confederates stepped up their attack, their enemy's retreat degenerated into a mad dash for safety. Soldiers and civilians were caught up in the panic, dropping their weapons and abandoning picnic hampers to speed their escape from the rebel guns. It was a rout.

Just as Confederate victory was assured, Jefferson Davis appeared at the battlefield. A military man himself, he could not wait for the result to reach Richmond, but came up to Manassas by train and horse. Seeing the enemy flee, Davis was anxious to order a savage pursuit, but his generals advised against it. In truth, the rebels were in no position to give chase. Johnston later said, "Our army was more disorganized by victory than that of the United States by defeat." Southern casualties numbered almost two thousand, while Union losses were closer to three thousand.

Elation and Despair

In the South, the mood was ecstatic. The press and the people were joined in thinking the war as good as over. The Yankees had shown they did not know how to fight, and despite all their material advantages, they were soundly beaten on the battlefield. One Georgia politician called Manassas "one of the decisive battles of the world" and felt sure that it had "secured" the South's independence. He was by no means alone in his opinion. Confidence was running so high that some began to wonder why the rebels did not "follow up the victory and take Washington," but most were content enough with the triumphant outcome.

Unsurprisingly, defeat at Manassas stunned the North. Everything that southerners rejoiced in, was cause for northern despair. One New Yorker, George

Templeton Strong wrote in his diary, "Today will be know as BLACK MONDAY. We are utterly and disgracefully routed, beaten, whipped." Horace Greeley, the *Tribune* editor whose jingoistic headlines had inflamed the Union and hurried the battle, was dejected. "On every brow sits sullen, scorching, black despair," he wrote. "If it is best for the country and for mankind that we make peace with the rebels, and on their own terms, do not shrink even from that."

Once the immediate gloom dissipated, and the realization came that the war was not going to be easy and glorious, but long, difficult, and destructive, a new determination rooted itself in the northern psyche. Lincoln himself was quick to shake off any despondency and set about the task of preserving the Union with renewed vigor. He ordered another recruitment drive for half-a-million three-year volunteers, and a few days later, another for a further half-a-million men. Lincoln also needed a new general to command them.

General McClellan

George McClellan seemed just the man that Lincoln needed. McClellan had already had a glittering career; he graduated second in his class at West Point, aged only nineteen, and he had been lauded for engineering work in the Mexican War. He had been chief engineer and president of railroads in his early thirties and had authored books on military strategy. And now at only thirty-four, Lincoln made him the second-ranking general in the United States, in command of the enormous new army, named the Army of the Potomac.

The northern public was looking for a hero to lead them to famous victory, and they thought they had

General George B. McClellan

found it in McClellan. The press adored him, and wherever he went people cheered and congratulated him, calling on him "to save the nation." Even the less excitable were impressed, and one level-headed diarist of the time wrote, "There is an indefinable *air of success* about him and something of the 'man of destiny'."

McClellan quickly set about restoring order to the defeated northern army, training the new recruits, ejecting unsuitable officers, and inculcating a new sense of discipline and pride. He proved to be an excellent organizer and administrator, and those under his command soon came to respect him, calling him "Little Mac" in endearment. The appreciative press described him as "Young Napoleon." The rag-tag collection of amateurs, inexpert militiamen, and volunteers were transformed into a proper army.

McClellan's meteoric rise, however, inflated his ego to unhealthy proportions as this letter to his wife reveals: "You have no idea how the men brighten up now when I go among them. I can see every eye glisten ... I believe they love me ... God has placed a great work in my hands ... I was called to it; my previous life seems to have been unwittingly directed to this great end."

McClellan was determined not to be forced into premature action, and wanted to bide his time and prepare his troops. Yet the longer the young general waited, the more cautious he seemed to become. He became convinced that Beauregard had amassed a vast army and was planning to attack. Supported by erroneous intelligence, McClellan thought his 120,000 soldiers were outnumbered by the rebels, when in truth he had well over twice their forces at his disposal. Self-confidence seemed to drain away from him, as did his will for action.

As the summer months of 1861 wore into fall, an impatience with McClellan was crystallizing in the North. This was exacerbated by the discovery of a "Quaker gun" – a decoy cannon made from a painted log – at an abandoned Confederate position near Washington, which brought doubt on his generous estimates of the enemy's strength. Pressure was mounting on McClellan to do something, anything to salvage northern pride before winter.

Ball's Bluff

Relenting a little under the strain, McClellan sent a small force toward Leesburg, some forty miles upstream from Washington to test the rebel soldiers

Yankees Under Fire

who had taken the area. One of the brigades was sent over the Potomac there, but was soon pinned down by Confederate troops stationed above on a steep bank known as Ball's Bluff. The Yankees failed to find cover, and many were killed or drowned as they tried to cross back over the river. Among the dead was Colonel Edward Baker, a close friend of Lincoln's, after whom the President had named his second son.

A second defeat so close to Washington caused another wave of shock and soul-searching, resulting in the foundation of the Joint Committee on the Conduct of the War, a body designed to ferret out the reasons, and persons, responsible for such failures. General Charles Stone was the scapegoat for the

Ball's Bluff humiliation, and without even a chance to defend himself, was incarcerated for more than six months.

Public pressure for a Union victory again started to mount, and Lincoln responded to it by trying to coax McClellan into action. He gave the general all he needed, and even removed the elderly General-in-Chief Winfield Scott to give McClellan command of all the armies. By November 1861, McClellan's forces and armaments were three times greater than the Confederates, but still he hesitated. He was tired of being harassed by politicians and had little time for the Republicans. In a letter to his wife he likened the cabinet to "geese," calling its various members anything from "a meddlesome, officious, incompetent little puppy" to "a garrulous old woman;" even the President did not escape McClellan's invective, referred to as "a well meaning baboon . . . 'the original gorilla.'"

Complaining bitterly that he could not move "without more means," McClellan resigned himself to a "winter of inactivity." As northern morale once again waned, he refused to take responsibility for his own caution, saying that he was "thwarted and deceived by incapables at every turn . . . The fault will not be mine; there will be that consolation for my conscience, even if the world at large never knows it."

Chapter Three

The War of the Water

I have now attained what I have been looking for all my life – a flag – and having attained it, all that is necessary to complete the scene is a victory. If I die in the attempt it will only be what every officer has to expect.

David Farragut

Blockades at Sea

While General McClellan vacillated in Washington, the United States Navy swiftly set about blockading 3500 miles of Confederate coastline. At the beginning of the war, the Union Navy only had a few dozen ships to patrol this vast expanse of shoreline, which included a number of heavily fortified southern ports and hundreds of labyrinthine inlets, islets, bays, and deltas to complicate the task. Compounding the problem, the navy only had control of two supply bases in the South, meaning its ships spent more time making the long runs to these bases than rounding up the blockade runners.

Clearly urgent work needed to be done to extend the US Navy's capabilities. To bolster numbers quickly, a hotchpotch of ocean-going vessels were called into service; it did not matter whether they were ferryboats or tourist steamboats, rickety old sailing brigs or tugboats. Each was given some kind of armament and set to the job of patrolling southern waters, putting the blockade into effect. New boats were also ordered that would suit the art of blockading better than anything that was currently held by the navy.

The Navy Yard, Washington, DC

This meant designing new craft that could cope with shallow inshore water, and vessels that could navigate the many networks of narrow rivers and tangled outlets where it might be impossible to turn round. Innovative new boats were created, such as the "double-ender," which was fully reversible, having pilot decks and rudders at both ends, and engines that could work both ways easily. Heavy, steam-powered gunboats were also constructed, which the northern shipyards were able to build from scratch in just three months. By December 1861, the navy had inflated its fleet to 264 vessels, and the number was set only to grow throughout the war years, far outstripping

Ironclad in Construction

their Confederate rivals. As the war progressed, the northern blockades would become increasingly important, gradually strangling vital southern supplies, goods, and resources from the armies – and people – that would desperately need them.

The Trent

As the blockade began to take shape in 1861, the Confederates hoped that the European powers – particularly the British – would deem it illegal. International law at that time stipulated that "blockades, in order to be binding, must be effective; that is to say, maintained by forces strong enough to prevent access." In the beginning, the US Navy was so small that the blockade was largely ineffective, and the South had every reason to expect the British to disregard it. Eventually, the rebels supposed, the British would even deploy the Royal Navy to guard merchant ships on trade runs.

The belief was still strong in the South that Britain would soon buckle under the pressure of having its cotton supplies cut off. However, the British had no intention of getting involved in the war, and neither would they succumb to the Confederacy's economic "bullying."

To press the Confederate cause further in Europe, Jefferson Davis sent two important representatives, James Mason and John Slidell, to London and Paris respectively. The diplomats slipped through the US blockade and at Havana boarded the British steamer, *Trent*. Suffering the double insult of British collusion with the southern "insurrectionists" and the failure of the blockade to capture Mason and Slidell, Captain Charles Wilkes took it upon himself to put the matter right; in doing so, he bought the United States and Britain to the brink of war.

Stationed in Cuba on his sloop USS *San Jacinto*, Wilkes fired some warning shots at the *Trent*, boarded it and captured the two Confederate diplomats, then sailed back to Boston, where he was received as a hero. In Britain, however, the reaction was outrage that this ignominy should have befallen a British ship. The Prime Minister, Lord Palmerston, told his cabinet, "You may stand for this, but damned if I will." An ultimatum was delivered to Washington demanding the release of the prisoners and an immediate apology. Meantime, a force of 11,000 troops were dispatched to Canada, and the British Atlantic fleet was mobilized.

Many Yankees welcomed another chance to go to war with the British, but Lincoln saw that such a thing was bound to overstretch his armies, and insisted it was best to wage "one war at a time." The United States duly backed down, releasing their trophy prisoners and apologizing, and a second war was averted.

Naval Offenses

In the summer of 1861, the navy was only managing to capture a tiny fraction of the rebel blockade runners. New bases along the Confederate coastline were needed if the blockade was to be effective.

Commodore Silas Stringham gathered seven ships and a couple of marine transports in an attempt to take Hatteras Inlet on the North Carolina coast. Near Hatteras were waterways holding vital communication links inland toward Richmond. Its capture would be a true thorn in the Confederate side.

Stringham's flotilla met with little difficulty on its approach to Hatteras, and his guns soon battered the unprepared fort into the ground. The small southern force posted there surrendered on August 29, and news of the capture was devoured hungrily by the victory-starved northern public.

Within a few weeks, a larger flotilla was assembled under the command of Flag Officer Samuel du Pont. The target was Port Royal, South Carolina, one of the best natural harbors on the southern Atlantic seaboard. On November 7, du Pont launched his attack, hurling shells at the two forts that guarded Port Royal Bay from his seventeen steam-powered warships. After a few hours of heavy bombardment, the rebels fled the forts and several thousand Union marines stormed in, securing the bay.

Further down the coast, southern naval weakness continued to be exploited with the fall of a number of

General Ambrose E. Burnside

small harbors such as St. Augustine in Florida, and Fort Pulaski which guarded the entrance to Savannah, Georgia.

A joint army and naval exhibition led by General Ambrose E. Burnside – the man who famously sported enormous muttonchop whiskers, spawning the term "sideburns" to describe them – was sent early in 1862 to take all the ports in North Carolina from the new acquisition at Hatteras Inlet, save for heavily-defended Wilmington. A brilliant amphibious assault combining the firepower of the gunboats and versatility of ground troops won Burnside Roanoke Island and its 2675 defenders at the cost of just over 250 casualties. Within a few weeks, Burnside had taken control of all the targeted ports and sounds in North Carolina, immeasurably increasing the success of the naval blockade and giving Davis the added headache of a possible land invasions from these points. Where the northern army had performed so dismally in Virginia, its navy was fostering an air of invincibility. For the Confederates, the shine from their great victory at Manassas was beginning to dull.

The Age of the Ironclads

After a string of Yankee successes at sea, it seemed that the rebels could do little to threaten Union naval superiority. The South did, however, have one trick up its sleeve that would revolutionize naval warfare.

When the war broke out, the Confederacy hardly had a fleet at all. The Federals had either seized or destroyed most of the warships based in the South at the outset. Even so, the rebels strove to make the most of what little they had, transforming wrecks into fearsome fighting machines. One such wreck was the *Merrimac*, a half-burned frigate, which they clad in layers of plate iron, equipped with ten hefty guns and renamed *Virginia*.

News that the rebels were building an ironclad warship sent chills of fear to the heart of Washington. The North decided it could not afford to let the rebels regain control of the coast with some devastating new super-weapon, so designers were commissioned to come up with their own ironclads. The best idea came from John Ericsson, who drew a plan for a ship cased in 4.5 inches of iron, which would sit low in the water, exposing just a couple of feet at most to enemy fire. The showpiece was a revolving turret protected by eight inches of armor plating, housing two eleven-inch guns, each capable of launching 175-pound shot. The government backed Ericsson's design and quickly went about building it. The *Monitor*, as he called it, was ready in January 1862, before the *Virginia* had even hit the water.

By March, however, the *Virginia* was finally ready to sail, and with its two old engines straining, it crawled out from Norfolk at a sluggish four knots, and headed off to Hampton Roads where the waters were tightly blockaded.

Before long, the ironclad had run into trouble – five Union ships patrolling the mouth of the James River. At last the new technology would be put to the

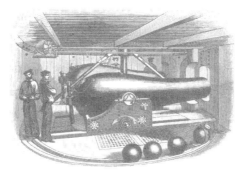

Gun Turret on an Ironclad

test. The *Virginia* first went for the *Cumberland*, a wooden sailing ship, unloading shells into its flimsy side before ramming it and tearing a hole in the hull, sinking it. Not satisfied with that display of power, the ironclad then made for the *Congress*, another wooden warship, launching broadside after broadside at it until it went up in flames. All the while, the Union fired with all its might, but their shells glanced off the *Virginia*'s low sloping sides with little effect. Worse still, the flagship of the five, the *Minnesota*, ran aground as it tried to maneuver into a better position.

The *Virginia*'s first day in service had been a total triumph. It sailed back to harbor, content to leave the

The Monitor *and the* Virginia

Minnesota for the next morning. In panic, the Federals quickly sent for *Monitor*, which had to weather a severe storm to get to the *Minnesota* that night from Brooklyn.

As dawn broke the *Virginia* returned to find a strange raft alongside the grounded ship. When this "raft" began to shoot off its huge guns at the *Virginia*, the southern crew were amazed. The *Monitor*, a far more nimble ship, circled its unwieldy enemy, launching shell after shell at it, but neither could break through their rival's iron armor. After a couple of hours of mutual bombardment, the crews realized it was a stalemate, and the *Virginia* limped back to Norfolk.

Neither ship fought again after this battle, but both

sides raced to build more ironclads. War at sea had been changed forever, and soldiers and marines alike would dread the presence of the enemy's armored ships for years to come.

The Western Theater

Military strategists on both sides soon realized that the control of the western rivers was at least as important as the naval blockade and control of the sea. In the nineteenth-century West, rivers were the freeways of the region, the crucial supply routes linking all the major towns. Roads were rarely better than bumpy dirt tracks, prone to flooding and often impassable for months of the year. Railroads were growing in importance, but at the time of the Civil War serviced relatively little of the West. William Tecumseh Sherman, who would go on to have unparalleled success in the West, foretold that "whatever nation gets . . . control of the Ohio, Mississippi, and Missouri will control the continent."

The Federals recognized that an amphibious force would be needed to conquer the West, neither riverboats nor infantries alone would prevail. The

General Albert Sidney Johnston

War Department ordered the construction of shallow-draft gunboats, specifically designed for river warfare, protected by thick iron, low-slung, and bristling with weapons.

The Confederates also understood the importance of defending their rivers. The Mississippi had been particularly heavily fortified, with a formidable stronghold at Columbus just fifteen miles south of the Union encampment at Cairo, Illinois. The rebel troops were under the command of General Albert Sidney Johnston, venerated by contemporaries as one of the sharpest military minds in the war. The Union appointed General Henry Halleck, a strategist of some renown, nicknamed "Old Brains," to command the West and General Don Carlos Buell to oversee territories east of the Cumberland River. Both

Halleck and Buell were shrewd organizers capable of making hardened fighting men out of green recruits in a short time. But like McClellan in Virginia, both were prone to hesitate rather than act – and neither enjoyed the thought of sharing command with the other.

Fortunately for the Union, Halleck had one of the best soldiers that the Civil War ever produced, a man who loved to attack, whose no-nonsense approach to battle inspired confidence and respect from his men. Brigadier General Ulysses S. Grant also possessed a keen understanding of any given military situation; he knew which course to take and how to take it. In this case he soon realized that while the Mississippi was strongly guarded, the Confederates had overlooked protecting the Tennessee and Cumber-

Brigadier General Ulysses S. Grant

land Rivers properly, waterways that penetrated not only prime agricultural and iron-producing land, but the heart of the Confederacy itself.

Grant urged Halleck to allow an attack on Fort Henry on the Tennessee. It appeared to be the weak link in Johnston's front, a fort unusually surrounded by high ground and prone to persistent flooding from the river. In January 1862, Halleck gave Grant permission to attack.

Unconditional Surrender

With 15,000 men and a number of river ironclads and gunboats, Grant gave orders to shell the fort from the river while infantry units surrounded it. As it happened, heavy rains had greatly slowed Grant's foot-soldiers, but also raised the river level, putting several of the fort's guns out of use. On February 6, the river boats reached the fort and began to hurl shells at its flimsy defenses. Before Grant's soldiers had even arrived, the rebels were forced to abandon the position and fled cross-country eastward to the better-defended Fort Donelson on the Cumberland.

Grant swung his troops round in pursuit, but further

rains hampered his advance. Meanwhile, his riverboats wreaked further havoc, destroying a rail bridge that connected the bulk of Johnston's eastern forces to Columbus, and sinking or seizing nine rebel ships.

Before the Union forces could launch an attack on Fort Donelson, Johnston quickly reinforced it with 12,000 men. Fort Donelson was in a far better position than Fort Henry, commanding a high bluff over the river and surrounded by three-mile trenches to hinder land attacks. Grant launched his offensive on February 14, employing a similar strategy as he used on the other fort a week earlier. This time, the gunboats were no match for the rebel artillery dug in to the bluff, but Grant still had the fort surrounded. Early next morning the Confederates made a brave attempt at bursting out, but Grant rallied his troops and held the rebels down. Fearing imminent defeat, two of the fort's three commanders slipped away during the night, leaving Simon Bolivar Buckner to face the music with the troops. At dawn Buckner sent a message to Grant asking for terms of surrender. The reply was characteristically brusque: "No terms except an unconditional and immediate surrender can be accepted. I propose to move immediately upon your works."

Storming a Fort from the Water

Buckner could do nothing but surrender the fort and its 13,000 men. It was the best news the North had had in months, and Grant became an overnight sensation. Lincoln wasted no time promoting him to major general while the press, playing on his initials, lauded him as "Unconditional Surrender Grant."

Shiloh

Grant's victories spelt strategic calamity for the South. The Union forces had driven a wedge between Johnston's armies at Columbus in the west and

Nashville in the east. The rebel commander had to evacuate both, much to the consternation of the Confederate public. Beauregard was sent from Virginia to aid Johnston, and between them, they managed to bring their disparate troops together from Columbus, Nashville, New Orleans, and Mobile, amassing around 50,000 men at Corinth, Mississippi. Corinth was a vital junction, where railroads linked Mobile to Ohio, and the West to Virginia.

Halleck, who had now been given command of all Union armies in the West, began gathering his 75,000-strong force to set against the rebels, calling Buell down from Nashville. Johnston soon saw that if he sat around for long, he would be badly outnumbered and reasoned that a surprise attack before Halleck and Buell had convened would be his best course of action. Grant had already encamped on the banks of the Tennessee, at Pittsburg Landing some twenty miles from Corinth. Luckily for Johnston, Grant was so geared up for his own offensive that he had not even considered that rebels might be planning an attack on him. His camp had no defenses and his watchmen were not posted more than a few hundred yards away from it, giving them little time to raise the alarm in an emergency.

On the morning of April 6, 1862, hordes of graycoats, all screaming the rebel yell, charged out of the forests around Shiloh Church upon the Federal camps. Brigadier General William Tecumseh Sherman mounted his horse to see what the fuss was about, and a shot whizzed by him, killing his orderly at his side. Throughout the day, Sherman proved to be a model commander, rallying his troops (for many it was their first taste of battle), riding up and down his lines even though he was twice wounded and had three horses shot beneath him. But Johnston's surprise attack was too much and Union troops began to disintegrate, falling back to the Tennessee River. Grant did his best to regroup stragglers into coherent lines of defense. On the other side, Johnston rode up to the front to encourage his weary men but was killed.

A heroic stand late in the day by Union soldiers at an area of sunken road known as the "hornets' nest," allowed Grant time to take high ground at the landing, and in the gathering dusk, Buell's brigade arrived at the river. This radically changed the balance of power and on the second day, Grant ordered an all-out counterattack against the exhausted and outnumbered Confederate troops.

Union Soldiers Defend Their Position

The fresh Union army pushed the graycoats back through the carnage and bodies of the previous day, until Beauregard was forced to order a retreat. The Federals were too tired to offer much of a pursuit.

The battle had been devastating on both sides. Although victorious, the Union had lost around 13,000 men, and the Confederates 10,700, making the Battle of Shiloh by far the bloodiest engagement there had ever been in America. Sadly, the scale of death and destruction at Shiloh was to become a matter of course later in the Civil War, but at the time, the number of casualties stunned both the Confederacy and the Union. In the North, the pain of it was quickly lessened by the joy of victory; after initial criticism for being taken by surprise, Grant was again hailed a hero, and Sherman too was singled

The Dead Awaiting Burial

out as a great prospect for the future. The South meanwhile descended into bitter recrimination. Jefferson Davis mourned the loss of his great friend Albert Sidney Johnston, and badly fell out with General Beauregard. Their sour relationship would go on to undermine crucial command decisions in the Confederacy.

The Fall of New Orleans

To heighten southern woes, the Confederates suffered a number of other defeats in the spring of 1862. Pea Ridge in Arkansas, and New Madrid and the stronghold Island Number Ten, both on the Mississippi, fell into Union hands. If that was not bad enough, Halleck rallied his armies after Shiloh and pushed on to Corinth with a force of 100,000 men, frightening Beauregard away. Of all these springtime defeats, none dealt more of a psychological blow to the South than the fall of New Orleans, the biggest city in the Confederacy.

Flag Officer David G. Farragut had command of a flotilla comprising nine sloops, fourteen gunboats, nineteen mortar schooners, capable of throwing 13-inch shells out of their enormous guns, and transports containing 15,000 troops. Sixty-year-old Farragut had spent a lifetime at sea, and served under the hero David Porter as a boy in the Anglo-American War of 1812, when he was placed in

Admiral David G. Farragut

command of a captured British ship aged only twelve.

In early April 1862, Farragut reached the mouth of the Mississippi, but several formidable obstacles lay between him and New Orleans: two oppressive forts – Jackson and St. Philip – and a string of hulks chained across the river. For a week, the Union mortar boats slung their massive shells at the forts from a safe distance, launching around 3000 of them each day. On the seventh day, Farragut decided it was time to press past the forts. Even though they had been savagely battered by the bombardment, the forts still had plenty of powerful guns at their disposal.

Under cover of nightfall on April 24, a vanguard group managed to sever the hulk chain and make a small gap in the river defenses while the rest of the flotilla chugged upstream. The rebels soon spotted them and the forts opened fire with unrelenting force. Rebel gunboats slunk out of the gloom and blazing fire-rafts were floated into the fray. Four Union boats went down, almost followed by Farragut's own, the *Hartford*, which caught fire and ran aground, but was saved by valiant efforts from her crew.

Demanding the Surrender of New Orleans

The bulk of the flotilla steamed on past the forts, demolished a weak Conderate fleet, and took New Orleans. The forts' garrisons duly surrendered and Federal ground troops occupied the city without confrontation to enforce Union rule. Most of the city's defenders had already been called away to fight at Shiloh, and the few that remained surrendered or deserted. For the South, the fall of New Orleans would prove disastrous.

Farragut continued up the Mississippi, taking Baton Rouge and Natchez without much problem. At Vicksburg, however, the last rebel stronghold on the Mississippi, his trail of success came to an end. The city's two-hundred-foot bluff over the river, topped by powerful batteries, was clearly too much for the Union fleet to tackle on its own. Farragut sailed back

A Rebel Vessel Explodes

downstream a hero, and was made the United States' first ever rear admiral.

Meanwhile Federal gunboats to the north surged down to Memphis, destroying a rebel fleet in hours, and taking the city in front of a crowd of thousands. The Union's victories in the first half of 1862 had won it 1000 miles of passable waterways and 50,000 square miles of southern territory. The Confederacy was virtually split in two, held together only by Vicksburg on the Mississippi. The war on the water – both at sea and on river – had been decisively won. But for the North, one worrying uncertainty remained: could General McClellan replicate this success back in Virginia?

Chapter Four

Rebels Defiant

*He who does something at the head of
one regiment, will eclipse him who
does nothing at the head of a hundred.*
Abraham Lincoln

Hesitancy

The thought of General George McClellan's fearsome Army of the Potomac, the largest, best-equipped force in America just a couple of days' march from Richmond, can only have sharpened the agony of the Confederate defeat in the West. Rebel troops in Virginia were outnumbered three to one, and the southern public anticipated further disasters near the capital.

Their gloomy predictions were not matched, however, by concomitant overconfidence in the North. Far from it – a sense of frustration and distrust with McClellan was getting more tangible by the day. His inactivity infuriated Lincoln and sparked off rumors from McClellan's political enemies that he was actually a Confederate sympathizer. Even the general's friend, the new Secretary of War, Edwin M. Stanton was downcast. "The champagne and oysters on the Potomac must be stopped. I will force this man McClellan to fight," he wrote.

Despite concerted efforts to prod McClellan into the offensive, including a General War Order which called for a full movement of land and sea forces on Washington's Birthday (February 22), McClellan

Edwin M. Stanton

still dithered. He hesitated in attacking Joseph Johnston's army at Manassas, believing it to be far larger than it actually was. Instead he proposed to take his army down to Fort Monroe at the tip of the Virginia Peninsula, and advance northward to Richmond, bypassing Johnston's forces.

Lincoln did not much like the idea. For one thing, it took the Army of the Potomac away from Washington and the logistical nightmare of moving so large a force could only lengthen the delay in action. The President thought that McClellan was "only shifting, and not surmounting a difficulty" and that he would find "the same enemy, and the same, or equal, intrenchments, at either place." Nevertheless, Lincoln reluctantly consented on condition that the general leave plenty of numbers back to guard the capital. McClellan agreed, but when leaders in Washington took a tally of numbers, they found far fewer than they expected. In response, they took a whole corps from the general's command and handed it to General McDowell, gave 23,000 men to General Nathaniel Banks in the Shenandoah Valley, and recalled General Frémont from retirement, allocating him troops in West Virginia. When the changes had been made, McClellan's invading force had been pared down from 150,000 to 100,000 men – a development he was very unhappy about.

Johnston, meanwhile, anticipated McClellan's plan and moved his troops out of Manassas. The North quickly took the post and were dismayed to see that the defenses were much weaker than McClellan had imagined; "Quaker" decoy guns littered the site, which could not have held more than 45,000 rebels. The northern press fell upon this as another sign of McClellan's unsuitability for the job. "Utterly dispirited, ashamed, and humiliated," one journalist wrote, "I return from this visit to the rebel stronghold, feeling that their retreat is our defeat." Lincoln responded to the criticism and removed McClellan from command of all the armies, limiting his control just to the Army of the Potomac.

The Peninsula Campaign Begins

The Army of the Potomac finally set out for the Peninsula on March 17, 1862. Progress was painfully slow once it reached land. A wet spring had turned roads into sticky bogs, and rivers raged where McClellan's maps showed there should be dry land. It took them till early April to reach the rebel defenses at Yorktown, where around 13,000 men readied themselves under the command of the flamboyant Major General John B. Magruder.

McClellan's reputation as a cautious soul went before him, and Magruder exploited it to the full. Ever the showman, the Confederate commander paraded his forces in every visible, but safe, spot, and maneuvered his artillery back and forth – even ordered his bands to play after dark. McClellan

Army Band in Full Swing

swallowed the bait and telegraphed Washington that he thought there were "probably not less than 100,000 men, and possibly more." He opted to lay siege to this great illusory foe and called for reinforcements.

Lincoln was distraught and quickly wrote to McClellan, "By delay the enemy will relatively gain upon you . . . It is indispensable to you that you strike a blow . . . The country will not fail to note – is now noting – that the present hesitation to move upon an entrenched enemy, is but the story of Manassas repeated . . . I have never written you . . . in greater kindness of feeling than now, nor with a fuller purpose to sustain you . . . But you must act."

But McClellan would not budge. Instead, he spent the next weeks stubbornly digging his army into enormous earthworks, and readied his impressive artillery for a bombardment. Joseph Johnston was overjoyed, commenting, "No one but McClellan could have hesitated to attack," and marched his army down to Yorktown to reinforce Magruder.

For a month McClellan constructed his fortifications, arranged his troops and hoisted his great guns into position; he would at last attack on May 5. Timing his move to perfection, Johnston ordered a heavy bombardment of the Federal position on May 4 and prepared to evacuate during the night. The next day – the day of the great Union push – the Confederates had completely vanished. Their camp lay deserted; Johnston had called a hasty retreat back toward Richmond. McClellan called it a "brilliant" victory, but much to Lincoln's annoyance, this great "success" had cost a month and allowed the rebels to find a better defensive spot without any loss.

For once McClellan was relatively swift in moving on, catching up with the rebel rear guard at Williamsburg. Here the Confederates fought a short and savage delaying action – the first test in battle that the mighty Army of the Potomac had ever had.

Attack on Confederate Line during the Peninsular Campaign

The Union had 2200 casualties, some 500 more than the rebels.

McClellan marched on, coming to within a few miles of the rebel capital. In panic, the Confederate Congress fled, inhabitants packed up their belongings and ran, but McClellan, still believing himself outnumbered, once again hesitated. He called for General McDowell's troops to come in support. Stanton, the War Secretary, could not believe his ears. "If he had a million men," he complained, "he would swear the enemy had two millions, and then he would sit down in the mud and yell for three."

The Shenandoah Valley

The prospect of McClellan's magnificent Army of the Potomac within miles of Richmond, being bolstered by a further 35,000 of General Irvin McDowell's men, made the Confederate's position look bleak indeed. But thanks to a series of brilliant tactical battles conducted by Stonewall Jackson in one of the Civil War's most impressive campaigns, McDowell's army never came.

The Confederates knew only too well how sensitive Washington had become to the worry of rebel attack, and sought to exploit Union anxiety ruthlessly. Jackson, a highly religious and eccentric man who was often seen chewing lemons to relieve his dyspepsia, favored strategies that would "always mystify, mislead and surprise the enemy." In May 1862, with an army of just 17,000, he set about doing exactly that.

He began by marching to the southern end of the Shenandoah Valley, crossing the Blue Ridge Mountains east and making sure he was seen by Union scouts who reported that he was on his way to Richmond. At Charlottesville, however, he loaded his force onto trains and whizzed back over the Blue Ridge to Staunton, from where his men trekked through the hills to the village of McDowell. Here the Stonewall Brigade deftly overcame some of Frémont's forces, deftly unraveling Union plans for Frémont to liberate eastern Tennessee.

Hiking on to the bottom of the valley, Jackson then sent a cavalry troop on a feint up the valley turnpike, completely hoodwinking Banks, who was waiting at Strasburg. Then the rebel force swung east, overrunning a Union outpost at Front Royal,

General John Charles Frémont

threatening to come crashing down on Banks's flank. Realizing his mistake, Banks quickly withdrew his men northward to his base at Winchester, hotly pursued by the Confederates. They met in battle there on May 25, and the heavily outnumbered bluecoats fled for the safety of the Potomac, leaving behind rich supplies of food and weaponry, not to mention 2000 prisoners.

When Lincoln heard about the loss of Front Royal, he ordered General McDowell to send his division (led by James Shields) to the valley, halting its advance to reinforce McClellan at Richmond. Meanwhile, Jackson's indomitable force marched further north, almost up to Harper's Ferry, in yet another feint, this time for an offensive across the Potomac. Lincoln wanted Frémont and Shields to

Rebel Soldiers on the Move

close in behind Jackson from east and west at Strasburg and crush this troublesome brigade. Even though Jackson was almost twice as distant from the town as the Federals, his troops, by this time used to covering huge distances in short amounts of time, steamed south, marching through the night to beat the Yankee pincers. They passed Strasburg before the Union forces reached them, and regrouped at Port Republic, at the far southern end of the valley to make a last stand in the valley before heading on to Richmond.

Jackson's campaign in the Shenandoah Valley was an exhibition of raw cunning, nerve, and tactical flair – a campaign that has been studied in military academies ever since. In a month, Jackson and his troops had tramped nearly 400 miles, had triumphed in five battles, all but one of which he had had the superior numbers, despite facing a combined Union force of 33,000. More so, he had hindered 60,000 Federal troops from reinforcing McClellan at Richmond. Of his own achievements, Jackson said, "He who does not see the hand of God in this is *blind*, sir, blind!"

General Robert E. Lee

Encamped near Richmond, McClellan's Army of the Potomac cautiously awaited the arrival of McDowell's men before launching an attack. The army had been divided in two by the raging Chickahominy River,

General Robert E. Lee

which had been swelled by the unusually strong May rains. Joseph Johnston saw a chance to attack, leaping on the weak left flank of the Federals to the south of the river at Seven Pines (Yankees called the battlefield Fair Oaks). It was a savage and confused confrontation, waged in dense thickets, deep mud and flooded pools. After two days of bitter fighting, the sides disengaged without any significant gains. The Union had lost 5000 men to the Confederacy's 6000, among them their commander, Johnston, who was seriously wounded and spirited away to recuperate.

Jefferson Davis called upon his military adviser, Robert E. Lee, to replace him. Johnston's response to this was double-edged: "The shot that struck me

down was the best ever fired for the Confederacy, for I possessed in no degree the confidence of the government, and now a man who does enjoy it will succeed me and be able to accomplish what I never could." Being as bad a judge of character as he was a judge of enemy numbers, McClellan was overjoyed at the change, thinking Lee "cautious and weak under grave responsibility . . . likely to be timid and irresolute in action" – a description that was actually far more accurate of himself.

Davis had made an excellent choice in Lee, who proved to be one of the most brilliant strategists in the Civil War. It had been Lee who had conceived the idea of the Shenandoah Valley campaign, even if Jackson had carried it out to perfection. And now he was to command the newly named Army of Northern Virginia, the Confederates' most important fighting force.

His first course was to summon all available information about his foe, and with this end he sent the gallant cavalryman, Brigadier General Jeb Stuart, to make a reconnaissance with 1200 horsemen. Stuart accomplished his task in spectacular style, storming outposts, burning supply wagons, appropriating Union stores, taking prisoners and weapons, and making a general nuisance of himself in a 150-mile ride right

Brigadier General Jeb Stuart

around McClellan's army. He returned to a hero's welcome and gave Lee all the information he needed to deal with the dithering Army of the Potomac.

The Seven Days' Battles

With the information gleaned from Stuart's daring reconnaissance, Lee recognized that McClellan had a weak point – his right flank, exposed and isolated to the north of the bloated Chickahominy River. He shifted the bulk of his army to the north to face it, dispatched orders that Jackson should hurry down to join him (bringing total forces for the attack to 85,000), and dug extensive earthworks in the area facing McClellan's front, so that a relatively small number of men could delay a possible Union counterattack.

The offensive, lasting from June 25 to July 1, became known as the Seven Days' campaign, a sequence of bloody battles that cost the Confederates dearly in numbers, but nevertheless succeeded in forcing McClellan back to the James River. The fighting proper began at Mechanicsville, where the Federals bravely fought off the rebel assault before Jackson could arrive in support. At Gaines' Mill, the clash was ferocious, but the graycoats broke the Union line at a cost of 9000 casualties, almost the same as had been lost by the South in two terrible days at Shiloh. At Savage's Station the next day, Yankees again only just staved off a rout with some determined rear guard fighting and at Glendale (also called Frayser's Farm) the day after, the rebels lost twice as many as the bluecoats, but forced them back to Malvern Hill, near the James River. It was here that Union guns made full use of their position, demolishing each Confederate unit as it advanced over open fields toward them. Again, the rebels lost more than twice the number of their enemy, and Union generals urged McClellan to counterattack. Flatly ignoring their advice, he ordered a retreat to

Union Soldiers in Action

the river instead, a move that one of his brigadiers thought an act of "cowardice or treason."

The Federals had enjoyed "victories" in all the battles except at Gaines' Mill, but in truth their offensive was in tatters, the Army of the Potomac broken and demoralized. In effect the overall winners of the Seven Days' were the Confederates – Richmond had been successfully defended and McClellan's Peninsula Campaign was over.

Thirty thousand men fell during the Seven Days' – more casualties than in all the battles in the West including Shiloh. Lee learnt much about his army during the campaign. Bad organization had

Artillerymen Fight to the Last

consistently led to confused orders, muddled charges and high casualties. He restructured the line of command, splitting the army into two corps under James Longstreet and Stonewall Jackson and turned the Army of Northern Virginia into a formidable fighting machine.

Meanwhile, Lincoln set about his own restructuring program. He ordered an evacuation of the Peninsula, before the entire army came down with dysentery, typhoid, and malaria, and made Henry Halleck the general in chief of the Union armies. The troops of Frémont, Banks and McDowell were brought together and handed over to the command of John Pope, a mean leader, unpopular with his men for all his boasting and cockiness. The President also called for 300,000 more men to enlist to help "crush the rebellion." Preparations were underway for some savage battles; Lincoln knew that the Old South, slavery, and the Confederacy would have to be destroyed if a new United States could be built in its stead.

Second Manassas/Bull Run

General Lee thought very little of the braggart Pope, but he did understand that if Pope were to combine his 50,000-strong force with McClellan's, then the Confederacy would be in serious trouble. To halt Pope's advance, Lee sent Jackson with 25,000 men northward. On August 9, Jackson's superior forces clashed with Pope's vanguard divisions at Cedar Mountain. The Yankees were driven back, but the main objective was to pull Pope's army away from McClellan's. Sure enough, Pope's ego had been bruised, and set himself the mean task of hunting down Jackson and his famous Stonewall Brigade. In another sleight of hand, Jackson evaded Pope's scouts, marched his men over fifty miles in two days and looted the Federal supplies at Manassas, before disappearing again in the wooded hills around the site of the first battle of Manassas.

Pope searched in vain, pushing his cavalry and infantry to their limits in the hunt, before stumbling on Jackson on August 29. The fighting was intense, and the rebels resorted to lobbing rocks and stones as their ammunition ran out, but managed to hold their ground nevertheless. Pope, in characteristic overconfidence, assumed that he had won a famous victory and sent a telegraph to Washington trumpeting his triumph. On the contrary, the Confederates were far from beaten; Lee and Longstreet had maneuvered their men up to join Jackson.

The next morning, Pope embarked on his "victory pursuit," and was taken totally by surprise when Longstreet sent his screaming divisions ploughing into the Union's left flank, driving the terrified Yankees back. The next day, Pope, downtrodden, was forced to call a retreat, and scurried back to the fortifications at Washington.

Lee's victory at Second Manassas had been stunning. Outnumbered by over 10,000, he had inflicted casualties of more than 16,000 on the

Union, while his army suffered less than two-thirds that number. In three months, Lee had prevented what had seemed inevitable; he had pushed back superior forces that seemed sure to take Richmond; he had beaten the troops that had come to its support; and he had transferred the theater of war from the outskirts of the Confederate capital to the outskirts of Washington. Lee was feted across the South as a hero. In contrast, Pope, his reputation in tatters, was removed from his post and sent to Minnesota to quell a Sioux uprising. His performance had been so disappointing that Lincoln saw fit to reinstate McClellan – at least "Little Mac," as he was affectionately known, was adored by his troops and might be able to cajole them into winning spirits.

Artillerymen Wait for Orders

Bloody Antietam

Seeing the Union side demoralized and disorganized, Lee decided to press home his advantage and invade the North. True, his 55,000-strong Army of Northern Virginia was ragged, dirty, tired, and hungry, but it was not in Lee's character to let such a fine opportunity of total victory slip through his fingers. In the West, the fortunes of war were swinging the Confederates' way with promising campaigns in Tennessee and Kentucky. The Federals were at their lowest ebb and one more decisive

Confederate victory – especially on northern soil – might well be enough to persuade European powers to recognize the Confederacy's independence.

In early September he ordered his bedraggled corps over the Potomac. His target was not Washington (her defences would be too strong for his diminished force) but Harrisburg in Pennsylvania, where he would be able to sever important rail links into the West. To do so, he needed to establish a supply line up the Shenandoah Valley, and that meant knocking out the Federal garrison at Harper's Ferry. Dividing his force in two, he sent Jackson off with that objective.

As soon as it was clear Lee was planning an invasion, Lincoln ordered McClellan to hunt and "destroy the rebel army." In most circumstances, it would have been unwise for Lee to split up his forces, but knowing McClellan to be cautious and considering the Army of the Potomac thoroughly dejected, he was prepared to take the risk. What Lee had not banked on, however, was one of his subordinates losing a copy of Lee's attack plans – and it falling into Union hands.

McClellan could not believe his luck. He now knew that the enemy was divided far apart and easy prey. He could destroy the Army of Northern Virginia and win the war. "Here is a paper with which if I cannot whip 'Bobbie Lee,' I will be willing to go home," he exclaimed. Even with this information, McClellan paused, wasting vital time, while news of his find filtered back to Lee.

The Confederates took up defensive positions around the town of Sharpsburg, by Antietam Creek, not far from the Potomac and, having taken Harper's Ferry, Jackson hurried back to regroup with Lee. If McClellan had launched an all-out attack there and then, the chances were that he would have scored a massive victory and greatly hastened the end of the war. Instead, he dithered again for a crucial day as he drew up his battle lines and methodically readied his troops for confrontation. The delay gave Jackson just enough time to reinforce Lee, doubling his forces and saving a crushing defeat.

On September 17th, 1862, the bitterest, bloodiest one-day battle of the entire Civil War was fought. At Antietam (the South called it Sharpsburg), McClellan launched a three-pronged offensive which would probably have prevailed, had he coordinated his attacks better, and followed up breakthroughs in the Confederate lines with

Union Troops at Antietam

punishing surges. General Burnside too, was disastrously slow in getting his men over the Antietam Creek, allowing Lee to maneuver his troops to shore up weak points.

The worst fighting was in the north at the "Cornfield," and in the center at a sunken road, the kingpin position in the rebel front. The graycoats courageously defended it for hours as thousands fell – the site was known since as "Bloody Lane." When Burnside finally pushed his men into the fray it looked hopeless for Lee, but at that moment A. P. Hill's division arrived from Harper's Ferry, dealing the Federal flank a thundering blow and driving them

back across the creek as night fell, bringing the battle to a close.

Both sides, horrified at the scenes of carnage they had witnessed, spent the next day facing each other in stunned silence, counting their losses. The destruction had been unprecedented – over 26,000 casualties, including around 6000 dead, four times the number lost by the United States on the first day of the D-Day invasion eighty-two years later. On September 19, Lee saw that his invasion was lost and headed back to Virginia.

Although he had lost a couple of thousand more men then Lee, McClellan had won an important strategic victory. He had squandered, however, a real chance to wipe out Lee's army altogether and was soon criticized further for letting the rebels escape.

Lincoln in McClellan's Tent at Antietam

Lincoln, again desperate, ordered his general to advance; McClellan did so reluctantly, stuttering and halting all the while, until he was too far behind Lee to act.

In November, Lincoln's patience with McClellan finally ran out and he replaced him with General Ambrose Burnside. McClellan made an emotional farewell to his great army; even Lee, understandably perhaps, was sad to see him go, saying, "He and I had come to understand each other so well."

The Emancipation Proclamation

While the war was being waged at sea and on rivers, in the East and in the West, the United States Congress still wrestled with the slavery issue. In April 1862, slavery was at last abolished in the District of Columbia, and in June, it was outlawed in the western territories also. Despite this progress, Lincoln was wary about railing against slavery too strongly too quickly – it was still a highly sensitive issue. For one thing, there was the Union Army itself. Racial prejudice was still endemic, and Lincoln could not be sure that the average soldier would be willing to lay down his life for the freedom of black slaves. Then there were the fragile border states – talking too loudly in favor of either abolition could push them into the Confederacy.

Lincoln had to walk a delicate line, and was careful to emphasize that the slavery argument remained secondary to preserving the Union: "My paramount object in this struggle is to save the Union, and is not either to save or to destroy slavery. If I could save the Union without freeing any slave, I would do it; if I could save it by freeing all the slaves, I would do it; and if I could save it by freeing some and leaving others alone, I would also do that."

But it increasingly appeared to the President that the Union would most easily be saved if slavery was abolished. Emancipation, he believed, would cripple the Confederate economy and keep European powers from rushing to the help of such an inhumane system. Once Lincoln had made his decision, all he needed was the appropriate moment to announce it, and the victory at Antietam gave him his opportunity. Five days after the battle (September 22, 1862), he issued the Emancipation Proclamation, which decreed that from January 1, 1863, all slaves in rebel states "shall be then, thenceforth, and forever free."

The Proclamation was at first met with mixed feelings in the North. To many it seemed nonsensical. As the London *Times* saw it, "Where he has no power Mr. Lincoln will set the negroes free; where he retains power he will consider them as slaves." Some abolitionists too, felt that it had not gone nearly far enough, since the border state slaves would remain so. But despite appearances, the effect the Proclamation had was utterly to change the character of the war. As the President had it, the Old South would be "destroyed and replaced by new propositions and ideas." The Federal armies would have more than the vague idea of "the Union" to rally behind – they would now be liberators fighting for that great thing, human freedom. And, to Lincoln's relief, the armies were happy with their new role. After all, they wanted to be rid of anything that gave the rebels strength.

Fredericksburg

General Ambrose Burnside was a reluctant successor to McClellan. He had little confidence in his own abilities as a general, even less so when put in command of the Union's finest troops, the Army of the Potomac. However, Burnside was determined to fulfill his duty as best he could, and this meant to move and attack where McClellan had only stuttered and paused.

His idea for an offensive would be to move to Fredericksburg on the Rappahannock River, from where he could set up supply links with the navy at Chesapeake Bay, and advance on Richmond. To be successful, he needed to cross the river, occupy the town and secure the heights behind it before Lee could get his army into position. Unfortunately,

Bombardment of Fredericksburg

Burnside had a talent for issuing ambiguous and misleading orders, and there was general confusion about his requests for pontoon bridges, resulting in a fortnight's delay.

This gave Lee all the time he needed to dig his men into the hills backing Fredericksburg, a virtually unassailable position commanding sweeping views of open fields leading down to the town. Burnside thought that the rebels would never expect an attack on Marye's Heights, the most heavily defended area behind the town – but the element of surprise was

Union Army Crosses the Rappahannock at Fredericksburg

only in the stupidity of his decision to do so. At dawn on the cold morning of December 13, the Federals launched their attack, streaming over the river on the pontoons and taking the town with relative ease. This early Federal success was part of the rebel plan – they were luring the Union troops into an horrific deathtrap.

Burnside sent wave after wave of bluecoats toward Marye's Heights, each one blown apart by a concentrated barrage of artillery and rifle fire. A stone wall lay at the bottom of the hill defended by four lines of rebel soldiers loading and discharging their guns so furiously that the Yankees could not get to within fifty yards of it. And still they charged into death. As one journalist had it, "It can hardly be in human nature for men to show more valor, or generals to manifest less judgment."

When darkness put an end to the fighting, nearly 13,000 Union soldiers lay dead or dying on the battlefield, over two times the number of rebel casualties. Burnside wept when he surveyed the destruction and proposed to lead a desperate attack himself, but was dissuaded by his officers. When the news of the terrible defeat broke in the North, Burnside gladly accepted responsibility for the disaster, but Lincoln also felt the pressure,

Fredericksburg

remarking, "If there is a worse place than Hell, I am in it."

For a few weeks the two armies glowered at each other in the cold across the river, until Burnside unwisely decided to have another crack at it, moving his army upstream. He wanted to take advantage of the dry winter weather, ford the Rappahannock and come down on Lee's flank, but as his army set out, three days of freezing rain transformed the roads into quagmires that sucked soldiers, horses and cannon to a sticky halt. The ignominy of the so-called "Mud March" was too much for Burnside who promptly offered his resignation to Lincoln. The President could do little but accept.

Bunrside's Mud March

Around the Camp Fire

Woeful Winter

For the North it was proving to be a miserable winter. A string of defeats, each sustaining large numbers of casualties, made some wonder whether the war was worth waging. Northern Democrats enjoyed a surge of support, exploiting failures on the battlefield, which they directly linked with Lincoln's administration, and whipping up concern about the Union becoming overrun with free slaves because of the Emancipation Proclamation – another Republican "disaster." In congressional elections, the Republicans suffered, losing Illinois, New York,

Ohio, Pennsylvania, and Indiana, as Christmas came, the morale of the Federal troops slumped, worsened for many by calls from many families to desert.

The most extreme anti-war Democrats – known disparagingly by their enemies as "Copperheads" – sought essentially to return the country to its pre-war state. The Copperheads were a constant source of irritation to the government, especially the outspoken Clement Vallandingham, a congressman for Ohio, who loudly called for soldiers to desert claiming that the South was invincible. His views landed him in a military court where he was convicted of treason and deported to the South. Democrats were appalled, but Lincoln's reply to their protestations was powerful: "Must I shoot a simple-minded soldier boy who deserts, while I must not touch a hair of the wily agitator who induces him to desert? I think that in such a case to silence the agitator and save the boy is not only constitutional but withal a great mercy." The Confederacy, it turned out, did not much want Vallandingham either, and he was removed to Canada.

News from the West was also discouraging, particularly in light of the string of victories the

Union armies had won in the spring. By summer all attacking momentum had been lost and the rebels were running amok with a spate of cavalry raids followed up by a major invasion of Kentucky under General Braxton Bragg. The Union was whisked from the jaws of defeat only by the timely arrival of Buell's forces when Bragg inexplicably paused at a crucial moment. The two met again at Perryville in October, a battle of poor judgment and slack leadership, as strewn with errors as the fields were with bodies. There were 7000 casualties during the indecisive confrontation.

Buell was relieved by General William S. Rosecrans, who chose to lead an assault on Bragg the day after Christmas. It was abandoned after a Confederate cavalry ambush decimated his supply

General William S. Rosecrans

Union Artillery

wagons and rounded up a thousand surprised bluecoats. At Murfreesboro on the Stones River, Rosecrans and Bragg clashed again in bitter fighting that saw out the old year and ushered in 1863. The rebels hit first and hit hard, driving the Yankees back several miles, and compressing their line into an arrowhead. The Union line eventually snapped, but onrushing Confederates ran straight into the range of fifty-eight Union guns that proceeded to pound them back, killing 1500 men in under an hour. When the fighting finished on January 2, both generals claimed victory, but their armies had been so battered that neither could convincingly prove their case. Bragg retreated when Union reinforcements came, perhaps giving Rosecrans a better claim, but the Yankees had lost a third of their troops – the highest proportion of any battle in the war – and were unable to pursue. In fact, Rosecrans' "victory" was so hollow that his army could not resume the offensive for over six months.

Chancellorsville

General "Fighting Joe" Hooker was the man selected to replace Burnside as commander of the Army of the Potomac. He may have had a dubious moral character – his headquarters were likened to "a combination of barroom and brothel" – but his sobriquet summed up what Lincoln was looking for in his general: a will to fight. The Union men

General "Fighting Joe" Hooker

immediately took to Hooker's style and responded well to his efforts to lift them out of the doldrums. He improved their rations and cleaned up their disgusting sanitary arrangements (almost all soldiers suffered from diarrhea or dysentery at some point and many hundreds had been killed by disease); he restructured the units, giving them their own insignia, and set up a specialized cavalry corps; and he allowed deserters to return unpunished. As winter turned to spring, the morale of the men was soaring. In Hooker's own words, it had become "the finest army on the planet." He and the Army of the Potomac were ready for an offensive.

Lee's 65,000 troops were still dug in at Fredericksburg, and Hooker, learning from Burnside's mistakes, saw that the Confederates would only be shifted if attacked at the unguarded left and rear. To do this he devised a grand-scale pincer movement, which would send a third of his 135,000-strong force to keep Lee busy at Fredericksburg front, while he would lead 75,000 men twenty-five miles up the Rappahannock, cross it, and bear down mercilessly on the rebel weak points. It sounded an excellent plan and in the beginning, at least, it went like clockwork. But a combination of

Hooker's personal deficiencies and Lee's bold intelligence snatched success from his grasp.

At the exact moment that Hooker needed his nerve most, it deserted him. Inexplicably, in a tangle of thickets, scrub, bogs, creeks, and gullies known as the Wilderness (near the tiny settlement of Chancellorsville), some miles short of the open ground he had originally chosen to hold position, he called his men to a halt. Defying the military tactical rule-book, Lee immediately seized the initiative, dividing his army into three in the face of a far superior force. A small group under Jubal Early was left to look after the defenses at Fredericksburg; around 20,000 went with him to face Hooker at Chancellorsville; and Stonewall Jackson went with the remaining men on a fourteen-mile march round to the badly exposed Union right flank. Just as the bluecoats were stirring their cooking pots on the evening of May 2, Jackson's men burst out of the brush from every direction, howling their rebel yell. The Federal flank was soon routed, fleeing two miles before night fell and Hooker had time to regroup.

Encouraged by his success, Jackson took the unusual decision to go on fighting in the moonlight. He rode into the darkness to make a brief

Chancellorsville

reconnaissance, but as he returned he was fired upon by his own men, taking two bullets in the arm. In the morning the arm had to be amputated. Lee was mortified. "He has lost his left arm, but I have lost my right," he said.

At daybreak, the Union forces under John Sedgwick charged across the river at Fredericksburg, eventually taking the stone wall at the foot of Marye's Heights – the scene of so many deaths the December before. Meanwhile, Hooker remained overcautious, withdrawing his men from a hard-won hilltop, from where rebel artillery proceeded to rain shells on them. A cannonball hit a pillar at Hooker's headquarters and knocked him unconscious. He was woozy for the rest of the day but refused to hand over command to a subordinate. Had he done so, a counterattack would probably have been ordered, but greatly shaken, Hooker ordered a retreat. Lee then turned his attention to the problem to his rear at Fredricksburg and took the bulk of his force to face Sedgwick, driving him back over the Rappahannock. He left only 25,000 behind to face Hooker's 75,000, but with his uncanny knack of reading his opponents' minds, he sensed that Hooker had given up. True enough, the Federal commander ordered a full withdrawal.

Lee had won a stunning victory, but the costs had been great. Seventeen thousand Union soldiers had fallen against thirteen thousand Confederates. Among the dead was the great Stonewall Jackson, who died of pneumonia a few days after his injury. He had been instrumental in winning so many battles and would prove to be an irreplaceable loss for the South.

Chapter Five

The Turn of the Tide

The present movement of General Lee will be of infinite value as disclosing the easy susceptibility of the North to invasion. Not even the Chinese are less prepared by previous habits of life and education for martial resistance than the Yankees. We can carry our armies far into the enemy's country, exacting peace by blows leveled at his vitals.

Richmond Examiner, 7 July 1863,
a Confederate newspaper

Grant's Travails

The Union performance in the East had been very discouraging to Lincoln, and as the Army of the Potomac recuperated after the disaster at Chancellorsville, attention turned to the West and Grant for any good news.

The object of Grant's desire was Vicksburg, a heavily fortified town on a high bluff overlooking the Mississippi River. The town was undoubtedly "the key" to the West and if the Federals could take it, they would both take full control of the Mississippi and sever the Confederacy in two. Winning it, however, would be no easy task. A fearsome array of Confederate artillery perched atop the bluff made the town all but invincible from river attack, as David Farragut had found in 1862. The only way to take it was by land from the east, but even this was fraught with peril, thanks to impressive rebel defenses, earthworks and fortifications around the town.

Grant and his trusted compatriot, General William Tecumseh Sherman, had already come to grief once trying to take Vicksburg at the close of 1862. Their attempted overland pincer movement faltered when Grant's supply base at Holly Springs,

Troops Fording a River

Mississippi, was obliterated by rebel cavalry attacks, forcing the general to cease his advance. Sherman carried on oblivious of Grant's halt, and making his way through treacherous swamps and marshes, attacked heavily defended bluffs at the Chickasaw Bayou. With losses totaling 1800 to the enemy's 200, Sherman called off the assault.

Grant and Sherman went back to the drawing board and hatched up several schemes that might crack the Vicksburg nut. To bypass this "Gibraltar of the West," they dug canals which failed to fill with water; they cut a levee between the Yazoo and the Mississippi but ran into the impregnable rebel Fort

Pemberton and had to turn back; and they attempted to navigate the labyrinthine creeks and tangled tree-choked waterways to the north, but the river fleet soon stuck fast in the narrow channels and only just managed to escape before the graycoats closed in.

These fruitless ventures of early 1863 achieved nothing but frustration for Grant and his troops, and an agitated northern press rounded on him, hinting that he was back on the bottle – in 1854 he had discharged himself from the army because of a drinking problem. Ignoring his critics, Grant thought again about his options and in March 1863 he came up with a risky last-ditched plan. He would march overland to the west of the Mississippi far beyond Vicksburg and the river fleet would run the gauntlet of the town's batteries to meet them. There, the boats would carry the soldiers across the mile-wide river, so that an overland campaign could begin from the south. The plan meant that his troops would be without supplies or reinforcements deep inside enemy territory – even the daring Sherman thought it too much of a gamble.

As Grant saw it, there was no choice. If Vicksburg was not soon taken, the morale of the western armies

General Ulysses S. Grant

would plumb new depths and bring the whole offensive to an end. And with the dispirited state of the eastern armies, failure to capture Vicksburg might sound the death knell for the northern war effort altogether. Risk was inevitable and necessary, and the success of the North rested on his shoulders.

The Vicksburg Campaign

In the spring of 1863, Grant and his army set off, making good progress through the mess of Louisiana bayous and swamps. His gunboats also began their dangerous journey, a hushed sail under the cover of darkness past the looming Vicksburg bluffs. Rebel guards saw them pass, and shells showered down from the cliffs onto the Union fleet. Even so, only one boat failed to make it through.

Grant then ordered a decoy attack north of Vicksburg, and sent Benjamin Grierson – a man who had overcome his antipathy for horses since being kicked in the head by one in his childhood, to become one of the Union's most accomplished troopers – on a dazzling series of cavalry raids to bamboozle and inconvenience the enemy as much as possible. In the confusion, Grant managed to slip his men over the Mississippi without hindrance.

Instead of heading north straight to Vicksburg, Grant saw that it would be wiser to head north-east to Jackson, where Joseph Johnston had a sizable force that could not be ignored. Unencumbered by supply trains, Grant's men stormed across country living off the land, knocking out rebel forces wherever they found them. On May 14, they sacked Jackson and pressed west to Vicksburg, mauling divisions of Johnston's and John Pemberton's (who had command at Vicksburg) forces on their way. When the remains of Pemberton's defeated troops stumbled back to Vicksburg, one resident was astounded at the "woeful sight": "Wan, hollow-eyed, ragged, foot-sore, bloody,

the men limped along unarmed . . . humanity in the last throes of endurance."

In seventeen days, Grant's men had marched 180 miles, won five engagements and inflicted over 7000 casualties at the cost of only 4000. Not wanting to lose the initiative, Grant chose to press on to Vicksburg without delay, and gave orders for an all-out offensive on May 19. The Federals charged with zeal at the rebel defenses, but a tornado of shot and musket balls roared out of the dense Vicksburg fortifications, checking their advance. Another assault was undertaken three days later, met with the same intense barrage of fire and the Yankees were once again repelled.

Grant saw these attempts were futile, called for reinforcements, which bolstered his force to 70,000,

Grant's Headquarters at Vicksburg

and gave orders to dig in — a siege would be the only way. Fifteen miles of Union trenches and gun placements strangled the town, pinning Pemberton in. Meanwhile, the river fleet kept up a relentless bombardment while ferrying supplies to the Federal soldiers.

For those trapped inside Vicksburg, Johnston's ragtag army of 30,000 mainly untrained troops was the only hope. But, faced with Grant's far superior forces, Johnston was reluctant to move and urged Pemberton to break out instead. Johnston had little idea how desperate the besieged had become. Food was getting so scarce that skinned rats and mules began appearing at the meat markets, while household pets went "missing." Persistent shelling sent families running for cover in makeshift caves crawling with rattlesnakes, and soldiers subsisting on meager rations grew sick and developed scurvy. There was no chance of a counterattack from Pemberton. The fall of Vicksburg – a disaster for the Confederacy – seemed inevitable.

Desperate Measures

Jefferson Davis was deeply alarmed about the impending loss of Vicksburg. In May, he summoned his generals to Richmond to discuss what, if anything, could be done. One suggestion was to send Longstreet to Mississippi to reinforce Johnston, but Lee claimed that such a move would be too little too late. Anyway, Lee had other plans for Longstreet. His idea was to invade Pennsylvania, taking the ravages of war out of Virginia into the North to intensify the conflict between Republicans and Copperheads while also drawing Grant away from his siege. If he scored a resounding victory, there was also every chance that the European powers would recognize the Confederacy as a nation. Perhaps, they would even

Jefferson Davis

take Washington and force independence. The boldness of Lee's plan was irresistible to Davis and his cabinet. They could see no other better solution, and if their great general, now famous round the globe for his tactical genius, thought it would work, they had no reason to doubt him.

Lee had 75,000 men to deploy, all pumped up with their own successes and wafting the air of invincibility that wins great campaigns. He split them into three corps, giving one to his "old warhorse," Longstreet, another to A. P. Hill, a dependable commander who never failed to arouse valor in his men, and the last — what would have been Stonewall Jackson's corps — to Richard Ewell, who had lost his leg at Second Manassas.

General Robert E. Lee

At the beginning of June, his proud Army of Northern Virginia started its march westward toward the Shenandoah Valley. The Union cavalry was sent to reconnoiter and clashed with enemy horsemen under Jeb Stuart at Brandy Station in the largest mounted battle in the war. Cavalry charges across open fields with thousands of sabers glinting in the summer sun raged for twelve hours. The outcome was indecisive, but Hooker had learnt that the enemy was on the move. Stuart felt piqued at being caught by "inferior" Federal horsemen, and set out on a daredevil reconnaissance drive to win back his reputation – as it turned out it was one act of bravery that only contributed to Confederate disaster.

The graycoat advance was impressive and relentless. Ewell's corps swept up the Shenandoah

Cavalry Charge at Brandy Station

Valley knocking out Union garrisons at Winchester and Martinsburg, and capturing 3,500 prisoners. As Hooker watched the rebel columns streak away, he suggested turning the Army of the Potomac south to take Richmond. Lincoln was adamant: "I think Lee's Army and not Richmond is your true objective point." The Union army slowly followed Lee out of Fredericksburg, being careful to stay between him and Washington. Lincoln urged Hooker to attack, but his general vacillated, claiming he was outnumbered and that he needed reinforcements – complaints that echoed McClellan's. The last thing Lincoln wanted was another McClellan at this crucial

General George Gordon Meade

stage, so he replaced Hooker with General George Gordon Meade, a man with a good fighting record. The swap made no difference to the army's morale – they were on home turf at last and were cheered on wherever they went.

Meanwhile, Lee continued his march into Pennsylvania, and had separated his three corps. This was according to plan, but Lee had still not heard any news from his "eyes and ears," Stuart, who had managed to cut himself off from his army. Lack of information meant Lee had no idea that the Union army had crossed the Potomac, that they were nearby aimed squarely at his flank, and that Hooker had been replaced by the altogether more aggressive Meade. When he eventually heard the news from one of Longstreet's scouts, he quickly sent couriers to gather his corps at Gettysburg, but Hill's divisions were already on their way — supposedly after a supply of shoes stored there. Unknown to them, the 93,500 men of the Army of the Potomac were also converging on the little town.

Gettysburg

To their surprise, as Hill's men reached the outskirts of town at dawn on July 1, 1863, they ran into pickets of the Union cavalry, a detachment from the bulk of Meade's army. Although heavily out-numbered, the Federal troopers fought a spirited delaying action until reinforcements could be brought in. Hill too hurled support groups into the fray. What had started off as a low-level raid was rapidly escalating into a major confrontation as more and more soldiers from both sides were sucked into the fighting. Before long Gettysburg would become the biggest, most important engagement in the Civil War.

Eventually, the Confederate numbers prevailed and drove the bluecoats scurrying back through the

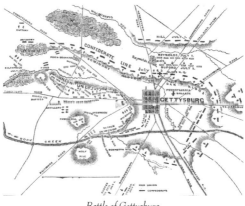

Battle of Gettysburg

streets of Gettysburg, delivering fire over their shoulders as they ran. Unwittingly the rebels were pushing them toward one of the best defensive positions in the area, Cemetery Hill. And waiting for the fleeing Yankees at the top was a fresh brigade already forming a strong line of defense.

By early evening, Lee had arrived at the scene and had had a little time to survey the land. He decided that he had no choice but to fight Meade at Gettysburg, but realized that he would have to remove the Federals from Cemetery Hill before the bulk of Meade's army arrived to make the position unassailable. As soon as Ewell reached town, he was given orders to attack the hill "if practicable." Stonewall Jackson, driven by a religious zeal to win, would probably have launched an immediate assault. But Ewell was no Jackson and chose not to move. The Federal line consequently strengthened, anchoring around Culp's Hill in the east and running along Cemetery Ridge to Little Round Top.

When Meade reached Gettysburg in the small hours of the next morning, he was pleased with his position along a three-mile hook-shaped ridge, and saw that he would be able to shift troops easily from one point to another, while Lee's men would have to march a long distance around him. Meade was happy to do battle here.

Lee, on the other hand, knew little about the area and had had only a short time to study it. He had not planned the major battle of his offensive here, but now saw it was too late to withdraw. And the longer he thought about it, the stronger the Union was getting. Lee resolved to attack as early as possible on July 2; Longstreet would take the Union left flank, Hill would hold the center and Ewell would make demonstrations on the right, leaning into a full attack should the Federal line weaken. Unfortunately, Longstreet's men

General James Longstreet

wasted crucial hours getting ready, and it was 4 p.m. before the call to charge could be given. When the yelling rebels steamed forward they smashed through Federals under Dan Sickles, who had disobeyed orders and pushed his men half-a-mile forward to high ground out of touch with the rest of the Union line, leaving himself vulnerable and Little Round Top undefended. The rebels pushed on, battering forward in an effort to take the unprotected hill, from where they realized their field guns could rain down shells along the length of the Yankee line. Sickles' men fought with grim resolve to keep them from it but soon collapsed, letting the graycoats swarm up the hill. Just as they raced up it, however, a Union brigade had taken position on the summit to defend. A bitter struggle ensued around the pockmarked, boulder-strewn

Rebels Push On

landscape, but eventually the rebels were pushed back. As darkness crept over the ridge, the bruised Union line remained firm.

The Third of July

The first two days of fighting had brought total casualties to almost 35,000 men between the two sides. In spite of this, both generals were on the whole encouraged. Lee felt that his indomitable army was on the brink of a famous victory. He felt sure he had weakened Meade's center and thought he could break it, while Ewell and the cavalry squeezed the Federal

Confederate Artillery

right and rear. Longstreet disapproved of the plan and thought it madness to push thousands of men over open fields toward a ridge bristling with guns. "General Lee," he reportedly said, "There never was a body of fifteen thousand men who could make that attack successfully." As it happened, Longstreet had great cause to be concerned. For, almost as if he had read Lee's mind, Meade told his generals, "If Lee attacks tomorrow, it will be in your front."

At 1 p.m. the rebels unleashed a ferocious artillery barrage on Cemetery Ridge. Some 159 guns poured shells over the Union center for over two hours, splitting boulders and sending shot and shrapnel

Confederate Charge at Gettysburg

flying. The Yankee guns responded and then fell silent. Thinking the enemy batteries destroyed, Longstreet readied his men and then begrudgingly gave the order for the charge. Almost 14,000 men moved out of the cover of the woods in silence, walking resolutely over the undulating hills, battle flags flying and weaponry flashing in the sunlight. It was a spectacular sight.

Then the Union guns let rip a devastating blow, firing shell and shot at the advancing gray line. The Federal batteries were very far from destroyed; they had merely been conserving ammunition for the rebel attack – and luring the foe into the open. Still the magnificent line advanced "with the step of men who believed themselves invincible," as one Yankee remembered it. "Solid shot ploughs huge lanes in their close columns [but] their shattered lines do not waver. With banners waving, with steady step, they sweep on like an irresistible wave of fate."

When the graycoats came within two hundred yards, the blues unloaded a furious barrage of fire on them, seventeen hundred rifles and eleven cannon going off in unison. "A moan went up from the field," one Federal officer recalled. The attack crumpled, rebel soldiers falling all around. Even so, General Armistead made it through the first Union lines at a stone wall with about 150 rebels. With his hat on his sword thrust high into the air, he urged his men to follow him over; only a few survived, and those that were not killed were captured.

Confederate Dead at Gettysburg

Less than half the Confederates involved in the assault made it back to their own lines. With tears welling in his eyes, Lee rode up to the returning survivors, telling them the disaster was his fault. He had lost the bloodiest battle in American history. He had also lost over 20,000 men and enough officers to cripple his command structure for the rest of the war. Meade and his army had also suffered heavy losses; between the two armies, over 6000 people lay dead on the fields around Gettysburg.

Lee's invasion was over. On July 4, the two sides faced each other in shocked silence counting their dead. And during the night, the remnants of Lee's defeated army skulked back to Virginia, their dreams of victory in tatters.

Union Dead at Gettysburg

Aftermath

"VICTORY! WATERLOO ECLIPSED!" trumpeted one northern newspaper after Gettysburg. The success had been monumental. And for the North the good news continued. The day after Meade's victory, Grant secured the surrender of Vicksburg, effectively splitting the Confederacy in two, and opening the sinewy length of the Mississippi to Union traffic. Lincoln was naturally overjoyed. The double blow to the South could only hasten the end of the war, and seriously weakened the position of the President's enemies in Washington, such as the Peace Democrats and the Copperheads. Better still, the European powers were now much less likely to intervene, and almost certainly would not recognize the Confederacy in its debilitated state. In fact, only one matter irked the President – that Meade had not followed up his victory by destroying the Army of Northern Virginia outright. True, Lee was no longer the super-hero people thought; his strategy was fallible and his army beatable. But while it was still at large, the war would drag on.

Lee himself was shattered by the dismal failure of his campaign, and tendered his resignation to

Jefferson Davis. Of course, Davis refused it. But the sense of gloom in the South was palpable. Most knew that the Confederacy would find it hard to bring itself back from the losses at Gettysburg and Vicksburg. The war had reached its turning point. As the diarist, George Templeton Strong wrote, "The charm of Robert Lee's invincibility is broken. The Army of the Potomac has at last found a general that can handle it, and has stood nobly up to its terrible work in spite of its long disheartening list of hard-fought failures." The Southern view was of utter despair. Josiah Gorgas, chief of Confederate ordnance noted, "Events have succeeded one another with disastrous rapidity. Yesterday we rode on the pinnacle of success — today absolute ruin seems to be our portion. The Confederacy totters to its destruction."

An Immortal Address

Four months after the Battle of Gettysburg, on November 19, 1863, Lincoln went to the town to dedicate a new cemetery there. A crowd of six thousand attended to hear the statesman, Edward Everett, an orator of great repute, speak about the

The Dead at Gettysburg

battle. Lincoln himself was only to offer a "few appropriate remarks" afterward. Everett spoke for two hours, and then the President stood up clutching in his hand the notes of his short speech. He began:

"Four score and seven years ago our fathers brought forth on this continent, a new nation, conceived in Liberty, and dedicated to the proposition that all men are created equal.

"Now we are engaged in a great civil war, testing whether that nation, or any nation so conceived and so dedicated, can long endure. We are met on a great battlefield of that war. We have come to dedicate a portion of that field, as a final resting place for those who here gave their lives that their nation might live. It is altogether fitting and proper that we should do this.

"But in a larger sense, we can not dedicate – we can not consecrate – we can not hallow this ground. The brave men, living or dead, who struggled here, have consecrated it, far beyond our poor power to add or detract. The world will little note, nor long remember, what we say here, but it can never forget what they did here. It is for us, the living, rather, to be dedicated here to the unfinished work which they who fought here have so nobly advanced. It is rather for us to be here dedicated to the great task remaining before us – that from these honored dead we take increased devotion to that cause for which they gave the last full measure of devotion – that we here highly resolve that these dead shall not have died in vain – that this nation, under God, shall have a new birth of freedom – and that government of the people, by the people, for the people, shall not perish from the earth."

Lincoln considered his address "a flat failure." But Edward Everett immediately recognized its brilliance. "I should be glad," he later wrote to the

Abraham Lincoln

President, "if I could flatter myself that I came as near to the central idea of the occasion, in two hours, as you did in two minutes."

The New Recruits

If Lee's army had still to be destroyed, the Union was going to need more troops, so Lincoln issued a draft call that July for 300,000 new recruits. Enrollment was enforced for all men between twenty and forty-five (in practice, those over thirty-five were likely to be exempted), and if inducted, would have to serve three years. There were ways that the healthy could dodge the draft: either pay a $300 commutation fee

The Draft

for each call-up (roughly the amount an unskilled laborer might earn in a year), or hire a substitute to take one's place. In poorer districts, this was understandably unpopular and denounced as "a rich man's bill." The Irish poor, struggling to make ends meet in the city slums, were particularly upset. They could see no reason why they should have to fight to free black men, who would only take their jobs from them at the end of the war.

On July 11, 1863, the first names were posted in New York, then printed in the papers rather insensitively alongside the names of the Gettysburg dead. An angry mob of Irish gathered in protest, and their demonstrations soon escalated into a full-blown riot. They ransacked the draft office, burnt the files, looted and wrecked shops. More than anything, it was black people that they wanted to hurt; they burnt a black orphanage and church and lynched a black man before torching him. The fifty-thousand rioters ruled the city for three days, until troops could be called in from Gettysburg to restore order. Over one hundred people were killed in the insurrection – most of them the rioters themselves.

While many whites were doing all they could to avoid the draft, black men were risking their lives to enlist. At the outbreak of the Civil War, black men hoping to join the Union army were turned away. Lincoln himself had said, "To arm the negroes would turn 50,000 bayonets from the loyal Border States against us that were for us." But by the end of 1862, the mood in Washington had changed radically. Committed to the Emancipation Proclamation, Lincoln had seriously been considering the possibility of arming black men, and had decided to create some experimental black regiments. Reports of their performance in the field were excellent: "No officer in this regiment now doubts that the key to the successful prosecution of this war lies in the unlimited employment of black troops." So in early

3rd US Colored Troops Banner

1863, Lincoln went ahead with a full-scale enlistment program. Many northern soldiers were still skeptical about arming blacks, though Grant was not one of them: "By arming the Negro we have added a powerful ally. They will make good soldiers and taking them from the enemy weakens him in the proportion they strengthen us."

On June 7, 1863, there was a significant conflict at Milliken's Bend, Louisiana involving black soldiers. After surveying the battleground after the clash, the Assistant Secretary of War wrote, "The bravery of the blacks completely revolutionized the sentiment of the army with regard to the employment of negro troops. I heard prominent officers who formerly in private had sneered at the idea of the negroes fighting express themselves after that as heartily in favor of it."

Many black soldiers were enlisted in the border states, the Union-occupied South, and the Confederacy proper — areas where joining up was the best means of gaining freedom. Of course, slaves running from South to Federal territory risked death. Huge numbers enlisted all the same. By the end of the war, around 180,000 black men served in northern armies, among them were the first soldiers to enter the fallen cities of Charleston and Richmond. Seventeen black soldiers were awarded Congressional Medals of Honor. Estimates have

Butler Medal

been made that the war was shortened by a year or more thanks to the Union's black troops.

In the highly racially divided climate of the Civil War, however, the new soldiers were badly discriminated against. In the beginning, black recruits were paid less than their white counterparts, given inferior clothes, food and equipment (pay was equalized in June 1864). Black regiments were often assigned menial duties and the hard labor that no-one else wanted to do. Medical care was also substandard, and the mortality rate for black soldiers was twice that of the rest of the army.

Nevertheless, the admission of black men into the army was one of the first steps on the long and rocky road to racial equality. As Frederick Douglass said, "Once let the black man get upon his person the brass letters, 'US,' let him get an eagle on his buttons and a musket on his shoulder and bullets in his pocket and there is no power on earth which can deny that he has earned the right to citizenship in the United States." To a black audience he implored, "I urge you to fly to arms and smite to death the power that would bury the Government and your liberty in the same hopeless grave. This is your golden opportunity." It was an opportunity that his contemporaries took with relish.

Chickamauga

For the moment it seemed that the Union had the Confederates whipped in the eastern and western theaters of Virginia and Mississippi. In the central areas, however, skirmishes, raids and the occasional clash of cavalry units had resolved little between the two sides. Lincoln was keen to take control of this region, particularly eastern Tennessee, where support for the Union was strong. Rosecrans' progress against Braxton Bragg's Army of Tennessee had been agonizingly slow, but early in July 1863, Rosecrans had also won another success to add to that of Vicksburg and Gettysburg in driving the Confederates eighty miles back to Chattanooga. At a broad loop in the Tennessee River, Chattanooga was the gateway to Georgia, the home state of many rebel war factories. At the crossroads of two important railroads also, the city would be a valuable prize.

In August, Rosecrans, with the help of Burnside, swamped the city with bluecoats, and drove Bragg out, without a shot being fired. The loss of Chattanooga was another hard knock for the Confederacy to take, and Jefferson Davis admitted that they were "now in the darkest hour of our political existence." Davis needed some magic to revive southern hopes and urged Bragg to concoct a strategy, promising him Longstreet and his 12,000 men in assistance. Bragg set about organizing a cunning ruse, and lured the bulk of Rosecrans' forces out of the city, pouncing on them at Chickamauga Creek.

Ferocious fighting over two days (September 19 and 20) made the battle the bloodiest in the western theater, with 4000 losing their lives and 35,000 casualties in all. A dreadful error by Rosecrans on the second day opened a massive hole in the Federal lines, into which Longstreet and his hardened veterans fortuitously rode. As the graycoats began pouring through the Union line, the Yankees fled in increasing

Confederate Line at Chickamauga

panic back to Chattanooga. General George Thomas made a brave delaying action, preventing Longstreet from turning the retreat into a rout, and winning him the title "the Rock of Chickamauga."

Longstreet was keen to follow up his success and requested reinforcements from Bragg, but Bragg was shaken by the heavy losses sustained on the field – thirty percent of his men – and denied him. Already an unpopular man with his subordinates (he was seen as a "merciless tyrant" who "loved to crush the spirit of his men"), Bragg's decision exasperated his officers, who eventually pleaded with Davis to replace him as commander. Davis did not like the two possible replacements any better – Joseph Johnston and Beauregard – and ignored their pleas. Bragg, meanwhile, began a siege of the city. The holed-up Federals only had a few meager supplies, and were slowly being starved into submission.

In October, Lincoln decided enough was enough, and put Ulysses S. Grant in charge of all western armies. Grant rushed to Chattanooga, replaced the stunned Rosecrans with Thomas, bashed a gap in the southern ring around the city and established a supply line. His presence was felt immediately. "When Grant arrived we began to see things move,"

Rebels Take the High Ground

one officer later remembered. Grant did not rest there, either. Reinforcements under Sherman and Hooker brought Grant's combined force to 72,000, outnumbering his enemy. The rebels held excellent positions on Missionary Ridge to the east and the towering heights of Lookout Mountain, but Grant resolved to knock them off their perches.

Chattanooga

"Fighting Joe" Hooker had the best of the first day of battle at Chattanooga on November 24. His troops pushed swiftly up Lookout Mountain, weaving through the boulders and pine that were wreathed in a thick fog. Emerging from the mists onto the surprised enemy, they forced the rebels to retreat to Missionary Ridge, and hoisted a large American flag on the summit, signaling their success in what came to be known as the "Battle above the Clouds." On the other flank, Sherman's men also fought well and took the high ground at the north end of Missionary Ridge, but neither general could follow up their gains further.

The following day, Grant ordered Thomas to advance against the rebel front and take a few of the rifle pits at the bottom of Missionary Ridge. Thomas's troops leapt at the chance to prove their worth after the humiliation of defeat at Chickamauga. A two-mile line of blue advanced over the open fields toward the Confederate dug outs in a maneuver that seemed to echo the disastrous rebel assault at Gettysburg. But amazingly, they took the first line of Confederate defenses with ease – and not content to rest on their laurels, took it upon themselves to sweep on all the way to the top of the ridge. Grant could not believe his eyes. "Who ordered those men up the ridge?" he demanded, but Thomas knew nothing about it. The generals expected catastrophe, but as they watched, their dread turned to awe. The torrent of blue burst through the Confederate line at its strongest point, past guns, muskets and bayonets, causing the rebels to flee in panic, and winning a miraculous victory for the Union.

Bragg retreated into Georgia and the war of the West was effectively lost to the South. What hope their success at Chickamauga had aroused was utterly extinguished. The loss of Chattanooga was an "incalculable disaster." "Unless something is done . . . we are irretrievably gone," wrote one southerner. But what could they do?

Cemetery at Chattanooga

Chapter Six

The Push for Victory

Grant is my man and I am his the rest of the war.

Abraham Lincoln

Grant in Control

At last Lincoln had found the fighting general he so badly needed. Ulysses S. Grant was a down-the-line soldier, a taciturn man who "habitually [wore] an expression as if he had determined to drive his head through a brick wall and was about to do it." His career had had its ups and downs, not least his ongoing battle with drink. In the 1850s he quit the army – he missed his young wife and children dearly and was regularly resorting to bourbon as solace. He then scraped a living where he could – bill collecting, selling firewood door-to-door in St. Louis and working in his father's leather store. One Christmas he had had to pawn his watch to afford presents for his family. But when the Civil War broke out he

Ulysses S. Grant

joined up again and quickly rose through the ranks, earning fame with his victory at Fort Donelson when the rest of the Union armies were being whipped by the Confederates. At Shiloh, his had drawn criticism for the heavy losses inflicted despite his success there. Some called for his removal, but Lincoln had already recognized Grant's value to the Union: "I can't spare this man," the President said. "He fights."

Grant had emerged as the greatest general in the United States, and on March 9, 1864, the government recognized this fact by making him lieutenant general (a post last held by George Washington) with command of all Union armies. Grant's task was clear: to destroy all Confederate forces. To do it, he planned to smash them in several places simultaneously and prevent rebel armies from reinforcing each other. In the West, William Tecumseh Sherman would attempt to crush Johnston's Army of Tennessee and take Atlanta, while "inflicting all the damage" possible "against their war resources." Nathaniel Banks would take Mobile and stop rebel detachments assisting Johnston.

For the Virginia theater, Grant designed a three-pronged offensive that would converge on

Richmond. Benjamin Butler would proceed up the James River, disrupt supply routes and menace the Confederate capital from the south; Franz Sigel would move down Shenandoah Valley, hampering Lee's communications; and George Gordon Meade would keep close to Lee, wearing him down at every opportunity. Grant himself would accompany Meade – effectively taking direct control of this most crucial part of the operation. At last, the Union had a far-sighted, coordinated plan, which used all its armies in concert. Lincoln was delighted.

In comparison, Lee's game plan was simple: play for a draw. He would need to frustrate all Grant's efforts to put his army out of action. He would need to get the best defensive positions and make Union attacks on his army as costly as possible. If the North began to feel that a decisive outcome was always out of reach, war weariness would set in and pressure would mount for peace and compromise. Furthermore, the presidential elections were approaching; if Lincoln lost to the Peace Democrats in November 1864, the Confederacy would have a far greater chance of achieving independence.

The Wilderness

The Union offensive got off to a dismal start. Banks, Butler and Sigel all suffered defeats and were forced to retreat – immediately putting Grant's grand design in jeopardy. Grant was not the kind of man to give up easily, however. His job of hunting Lee down would be more difficult – but not impossible.

The two generals' armies had spent the winter on opposite sides of the Rapidan River. In May 1864, Grant's Army of the Potomac, numbering 115,000 men, crossed the river and began marching south through the terrible tangle of oak and pine thickets known as the Wilderness, where Joe Hooker had come to such grief a year earlier. Grant was aiming

Hauling a Cannon Through the Wilderness

Fighting in the Forest

for the clear ground beyond where he hoped to give battle. Lee, on the other hand, with only 64,000 men at his disposal, had no intention of affording Grant that luxury, and pressed his forces straight into the thick of the Wilderness.

On May 5, a titanic battle broke out in that inhospitable terrain. The underbrush was so dense that "no-one could see the fight fifty feet from him." As one soldier recalled, "It was a blind and bloody hunt to the death, in bewildering thickets, rather than a battle." In all the confusion, men got lost and troops opened fire on their own units. The scrub caught fire, sending palls of smoke and making it harder to navigate; many fallen wounded were burnt to death.

The fighting continued for two days. Both sides'

lines had almost collapsed, but by the end, the Confederates had had the better of it. Lee had successfully neutralized the Union advantage in numbers and its heavy artillery that could not be used or maneuvered amid the tangle of briars and ground so rife with gullies and creeks. Grant had gained no ground, and lost more than 17,000 men – as bad as Hooker's defeat here. The Army of the Potomac was despondent, and waited for the call to retreat. But Grant was like no general that army had known.

As night fell, Grant commanded his men to continue the march south, saying, "Whatever happens we will not retreat." The Army of the Potomac was bruised, but it was not beaten. Morale immediately lifted and the soldiers began to sing.

Spotsylvania

Grant's objective was to take the crossroads at Spotsylvania Court House and block Lee's route to Richmond, putting him on the offensive. Lee, as ever the master strategist, had foreseen Grant's plan and had "already made arrangements."

When Grant reached Spotsylvania, he found that

Lee was waiting for him – his forces had dug trenches and breastworks, and were ready for an attack. In spite of this, during the heavy rain of May 12, Grant hurled 20,000 men at a salient in the Confederate center. Ranks of Union soldiers charged the trenches howling at the top of their voices, and overrunning them. Suddenly, it looked as if Grant had the breakthrough he needed to inflict serious damage on the Army of Northern Virginia. Lee himself saw no other solution but to lead a counterattack, but his men would not let him, shouting, "Lee to the rear! Lee to the rear!" and forced him behind to safety. The rebels went on to take their defenses back and stabilize the line, but furious fighting continued. The worst of it was at the "Bloody Angle" where soldiers

Confederate Sharpshooter

unloaded their bayoneted rifles in their enemy's faces and then once empty threw them like spears into the fray. The raking of gunshot around the trenches was so severe that an oak tree almost two foot thick was cut in two. To one Union soldier, it was "the most terrible day I have ever lived."

Darkness had long drawn in before Lee gave the order to withdraw to new defenses half a mile to the rear. In all, almost 12,000 soldiers had fallen at Spotsylvania, many of them at the Bloody Angle. One general surveyed the carnage the next morning: "At dawn we could see that the enemy's dead . . . were piled upon each other in some places four layers deep, exhibiting every ghastly phase of mutilation. Below the mass of fast-decaying corpses, the convulsive twitching of limbs . . . showed that there were wounded men still alive . . . The place was well named the 'Bloody Angle'."

Cold Harbor

For the next several days, Grant tried repeatedly to break Lee's grip on Spotsylvania through sequences of minor assaults and flanking maneuvers.

Frustrated by lack of success, the Union commander again ordered a move further south and east toward Richmond. As Lee raced to head him off, the armies clashed at the North Anna River and again at Totopotomy Creek. The big strategic position nearby was Cold Harbor, a crossroads near the Chickahominy River only ten miles from the Confederate capital. With the advantage of interior lines, Lee yet again beat Grant to the battlefield, and entrenched his 59,000 troops – almost half the number of Federals bearing down on him.

A fortnight of exhausting battle, movement and skirmishing had worn down the soldiers on both sides. The southerners were running low on food and supplies; constant firing, maneuvering, and digging in had sapped the mental fortitude of everyone. One Union officer later remarked, "Many a man has gone crazy since this campaign began from the terrible pressure on mind and body." Grant was sure his better-fed and clothed troops had the upper hand; he began to see Cold Harbor as his great opportunity to crush the rebel line and get the war over with. In truth, he was probably as tired as his men – even Lee had fallen ill for a week – and losing patience with this savage and protracted campaign. The temptation of an all-out frontal assault that might win the war was too much for him to resist. His more experienced soldiers could sense it coming; as night fell on June 2, they wrote their names and addresses on slips of paper and pinned them to their jackets, "so that their bodies might be recognized and their fate made known to their families at home."

At dawn the next morning, the Union assault began as thousands of bluecoats advanced on the formidable rebel trenches. The Confederates silently waited until the enemy was well within range — and then discharged a vicious barrage of artillery and musket fire. Riddled bodies fell, puffs of blood and dust bursting out of their tunics as shot and shell ripped across the blue lines. In a matter of minutes

Cold Harbor

thousands of Union soldiers lay in front of the rebel earthworks dead or dying; by the early afternoon 7000 men had been lost to around a thousand Confederates and Grant halted the attack, confessing that any further assaults would be futile. He realized that he had been wrong, but was too proud to call a truce to gather the wounded and inter the dead. For three days the bodies festered and the wounded perished in the heat of the summer sun. One rebel officer commented later, "The stench from the dead between our line and theirs was . . . so nauseating that it was almost unendurable; but we had the advantage, as the wind carried it away from us to them. The dead covered more than five acres of ground about as thickly as they could be laid."

Grant drew savage criticism in the North for the waste of human life at Cold Harbor. In less than a month of his Virginia campaign, he had lost 55,000 men. The press christened him "The Butcher" and questioned his "callous indifference" and "reckless insanity." But Grant was too thick-skinned to care what people thought of his tactics. Lee's losses had been great too – around 32,000 – and proportionately heavier. While Grant kept receiving new recruits, food, and supplies, he knew he had Lee on the defensive.

Petersburg

Ten days after the massacre at Cold Harbor, Grant was once again on the move. Up till now, Lee had managed to read all of Grant's intentions, but this time he was fooled by a series of Union feints toward Richmond. He had not suspected that Grant was moving the bulk of his forces south across the James River by virtue of a seven-hundred-yard pontoon bridge thrown up by his engineers in a matter of hours. The Federals were advancing on Petersburg, a town to the south of Richmond, through which railroads fed the capital with supplies. Manned only with a force of 2500 under General Beauregard, Grant hoped he could overwhelm Petersburg and choke Richmond into submission.

A Union vanguard of 16,000 under General "Baldy" Smith, reached the town on June 15 and launched an assault in the late afternoon. By nighttime, Petersburg was "all but captured." The moon shone down on the town and Smith was urged to clinch the victory; but to everyone's disappointment (including his troops) he demurred, balking at the thought of another Cold Harbor. The lost hours gave the Confederates vital time to reinforce, and over the next three days the Yankees failed to capitalize on their advantage. Meantime, at Confederate headquarters the penny dropped about Grant's scheme and by June 18, when 70,000 bluecoats had assembled at the outskirts of the town, Lee had arrived and dug his troops in.

The Cold Harbor disaster was still fresh in the Yankees' memories and the few charges made against the rebel trenches at Petersburg were at best half-hearted; many units were reluctant to move at all. The Federal commanders eventually got the message and ordered their troops to dig in for a siege. As the summer wore on, the trenches on both sides grew and grew, until they were a warren of twisting ditches and dug outs, bristling like porcupines with sharpened stakes to keep the enemy at bay.

Grant kept the pressure on Lee whenever he could, lobbing shells into the rebel trenches, probing weak spots and instigating skirmishes that continued deplete Confederate numbers. The hapless General Burnside came up with a harebrained scheme of his own – to dig a 512-foot tunnel reaching beneath the rebel trenches, then stuff it with four tons of gunpowder. When it was detonated on July 30, it sent an "immense mushroom" into the air which fell "in a

Union Artillery at Petersburg

rain of earth mixed with rocks, with beams, timbers, and mangled human bodies" and left an enormous crater 30 feet deep and 170 feet wide. The much-derided plan looked like it was actually working, but a mix-up in orders at the last moment meant that the accompanying infantry assault was over an hour late in coming – and led by James Ledlie, an incompetent officer with a weakness for liquor. Instead of sweeping down on the terrified rebels either side of the crater, the bluecoats poured straight into it where they promptly found they could go no further. The rebels regrouped and counterattacked, easily picking off the blues caught in the hole. Many white troops surrendered and were captured; the black soldiers caught had no such treatment and were murdered. As the disaster unfolded, Ledlie sat ensconced behind the Union lines getting drunk on rum. The so-called "Battle of the Crater" cost the Grant over 4000 men. He called it a "stupendous failure," "the saddest affair" he had witnessed in the war, and removed both Ledlie and Burnside from command.

After the crater, the northern press again criticized Grant and his "derailed" campaign, questioning the merits of the war. Democratic newspapers in particular whipped up anti-war sentiment with comments such as: "Each hour is but sinking us deeper into bankruptcy and desolation."

Reports of this could only have encouraged Lee. He knew his time was limited at Petersburg. He was pinned down – abandonment of the town would

Bodies in the Petersburg Trenches

mean the fall of Richmond – but he had neither the men nor the resources to break out. The Union presidential elections, however, were looming and might provide the means for Confederate salvation if the war-weary North would only vote Lincoln out and call a cease-fire.

Meanwhile Grant made the most of the situation. His campaign may have been executed at staggering cost (some 60,000 Union men had fallen), but he had kept Lee constantly on the defensive and had him under siege within a stone's throw of the rebel capital. With Lee immobilized, he could cause mischief elsewhere, not least the Shenandoah Valley, long the source of pain to the Union – and supplies for the Army of Northern Virginia.

Struggle for the Valley

Throughout the war, the Shenandoah Valley had been a thorn in the Union side. The Federals had consistently failed to keep the Valley out of rebel hands. Franz Sigel, charged by Grant with winning it back, had been defeated at the hands of a group of teenage cadets, amongst others. To make amends

Grant sent General David Hunter, a gruff and humorless man, to take over. Hunter quickly put the graycoats to rout during a ten-hour clash at Piedmont, killing their commander and storming through Staunton and Lexington, before turning on Lynchburg.

Lee acted swiftly to save the valley, dispatching Jubal Early with the Stonewall Brigade (the veterans of Jackson's great campaign two years earlier) to see off Hunter's threat. Early and his spirited corps drove the Yankees from Lynchburg, forcing them into the mountains of West Virginia – leaving the valley clear for Early to menace Maryland and Washington as Jackson had done.

Showing his usual dogged determination to see a job done, Grant's reply was to send General Philip Sheridan, a man with a true lust for fighting, along

General Philip Sheridan

with 41,000 soldiers into the fray, with orders to hound Early "to the death" and "eat up" the Shenandoah "clear and clean, so that crows flying over it for the balance of the season will have to carry their provender with them." Early was overwhelmed by Sheridan's horde and was squeezed up the valley after clashes at Winchester and Fisher's Hill.

Fearsome "Old Jube" was not going to go quietly, however. While Sheridan was away from his troops for a meeting in Washington, Early launched a devastating surprise attack at Cedar Creek, smashing through the Federal flank and putting thousands of Yankees to panic-stricken flight. Sheridan heard the commotion and galloped apace to the battlefield on his black steed. The sight of their leader immediately lifted the morale of the fleeing bluecoats; they rallied,

General Jubal A. Early

regrouped, and stormed back at the Confederates to snatch an important victory. Early and his dilapidated force retreated from the valley, so marking the end of rebel strength there, and Sheridan set about laying waste to the land. They torched barns and haystacks, demolished mills and machinery; they slaughtered sheep and drove livestock off the land. The "breadbasket of the Confederacy" was picked bare and would supply the southern troops no more. It was just the boost Lincoln needed before the elections in fall. Grant bombarded the rebel trenches at Petersburg to celebrate.

Prison Camps

At the beginning of the war, both sides agreed to a simple and efficient means of dealing with captured soldiers. Prisoners were often handed back "on parole" – that is, on condition that they returned home and did not bear arms until arrangements had been made for their formal exchange. Sometimes it was simpler still for rival armies to exchange equal numbers of prisoners there and then after a battle.

The system was all to break down at the start of

Confederate Prisoners at Gettysburg

1863, when the Emancipation Proclamation came into effect and black soldiers enlisted into the Union armies. The Confederates were willing to exchange black men who were free when they joined up, but refused absolutely to return escaped slaves – "contrabands" – whom they viewed as property regained. In practice, all black prisoners were either sent back to their old masters, sold into slavery, or killed. Some terrible atrocities were committed – at Fort Pillow in April 1864, for instance, hundreds of black prisoners were murdered while they begged for mercy. The Confederate commander at the scene, the daring cavalryman, Nathan Bedford Forrest (known as the "Wizard of the Saddle", and, coincidentally, the first Imperial Wizard of the Ku Klux Klan after the war), was unmoved by his actions and said, "It is hoped that these facts will demonstrate to the northern people that negro soldiers cannot cope with Southerners."

Shortly after this massacre, the Union recoiled from the parole and exchange system. Grant himself said it would not be reinstated until "no distinction whatever would be made in the exchange between white and colored prisoners."

The breakdown meant that there was suddenly an urgent need to accommodate thousands of prisoners, North and South. Shoddily built camps and compounds sprang up, often in great haste and in unsuitable locations. In both sections conditions were bad, but in the South where supplies were scarce and food running short, they were appalling.

Andersonville prison camp in south-west Georgia had the worst reputation of all of them. In the sweltering August of 1864, it had 33,000 inmates crammed inside its perimeter fence, each prisoner having less than six feet square to call his own. The paltry rations amounted to a few spoonfuls of beans, a pinch of salt and a mug of cornmeal each day; drinking water came from the idyllic-sounding Sweet Water Branch, in reality, a near stagnant streak of scummy water that also serviced the camp's latrines. Disease was rife, and men dropped dead every hour, their weakened, malnourished bodies unable to put up any kind of defense. Images of escaped prisoners, terribly emaciated with sunken eyes and hollow cheeks, leaked to the North outraged the people, but little could be done to end the impasse.

One third of Andersonville's prisoners – some 13,000 people – died inside its bounds. In total, 56,000 American soldiers did not survive internment in the prisoner-of-war camps. The horror continued until January 1865, when the Confederates relented and agreed to exchange all prisoners, black and white. As it happened, they had just decided to start using black soldiers themselves. After the war, Captain Henry Wirz, the man in charge of Andersonville, was found guilty of "murder in violation of the laws and customs of war" and hanged on November 10, 1865.

Sherman's March South

While Grant had Lee caught in Petersburg, William Tecumseh Sherman, his best lieutenant and trusted friend, was charged with a crucial element of the

General William T. Sherman

Union plan. He was to capture Atlanta, Georgia, a vital industrial center for the southern war effort. In doing so, Sherman would have to beat Joseph Johnston and his Armies of the Tennessee and Mississippi. "Uncle Billy" Sherman was rumpled and skittish, a man with a voracious appetite and a slight build, who paced around in his faded old blue trousers and talked incessantly on every subject. He, like Grant, had a passion for action and would not hesitate to take chances if victory was the reward.

The odds were against Johnston – he was outnumbered two to one by a better-equipped army. He could do little but make a slow retreat and hamper Sherman's progress wherever possible. Backing away bit by bit, the Confederates tore up railroads, burnt bridges and fought the occasional delaying action from

behind sturdy entrenchments. As Sherman followed, his engineers expertly replaced the damaged bridges and rail lines while his soldiers prized the rebels out of their defenses. Even so, the Yankee advance was painfully slow and Sherman was losing his patience.

By the end of June, Johnston had taken position on Kennesaw Mountain, not twenty miles from Atlanta. Sherman attempted to beat his foe with a series of frontal assaults, but the formidable rebel breastworks were too much and thousands of bluecoats fell in the stifling heat of June 27. As bullets and shot raged all around them, a rebel marveled at the way they "seemed to walk up and take death as coolly as if they were automatic or wooden men." Sherman never made this mistake again, and reverted to pushing Johnston back through feints and outflanking thrusts to the Atlanta defenses.

The politicians in Richmond watched Johnston's slow retreat to Atlanta with increasing concern. The "Gate City of the South" must not fall. Its loss, Jefferson Davis warned, would "open the way for the Federal Army to the Gulf on the one hand, and to Charleston on the other, and close up those rich granaries from which Lee's armies are supplied. It would give them control of our network of railways and thus paralyze our efforts." It was no secret that Davis disliked Johnston, and under pressure from his cabinet and military adviser, Braxton Bragg, replaced Johnston for General John B. Hood, a gallant soldier whose valor in battle had left him without a leg and the use of an arm. He was a fine aggressive officer, but Lee questioned whether he had the expertise to command an army — to Lee, he was "all lion" but "none of the fox." Lee's judgment of character, once again, proved correct.

The Fall of Atlanta

Sherman himself was overjoyed that Hood had been appointed; he liked the thought of imminent battle with the hot-blooded "Old Woodenhead," as Hood was

General J. B. Hood

known. Within a couple of days of receiving command, Hood impetuously launched an assault on Sherman's flank at Peach Tree Creek – and was beaten back to Atlanta's defenses with heavy losses. Despite this, Hood initiated fresh attacks east of the city in the following days; again he was repulsed at the cost of 8000 men. The Federals lost around half that number, but the promising young general, James McPherson, a close friend of Sherman's, was among them.

Sherman now planned to encircle the city, cutting off all of Hood's supply and communication lines. As the bluecoats moved in on the main railroad leading south of Atlanta, Hood fought desperate actions to keep it in Confederate hands, again suffering high numbers of casualties. For a month, Sherman probed and pushed, constantly threatening the rail line, while bombarding the besieged city. At the end of August, Sherman flung his troops once more at the railroad near Jonesboro, twenty miles to the south. Hood tried to stop him but was crushed, and was forced to abandon Atlanta or lose his entire army. The rebels burnt everything as they fled, and on September 2, Sherman's triumphant troops marched into the city.

News of the victory had an electrifying effect in the North. The stalemate in Virginia had frustrated the northern public, and the clamor for an end to the war was growing stronger by the day, but Sherman's success reversed all that. Hailed as a hero, one-hundred-gun salutes went off in Sherman's honor across the North. The Confederacy had surrendered one of its chief manufacturing and communications centers – a numbing blow. The southern diarist Mary Chestnut wrote, "Since Atlanta I have felt as if all were dead within me, forever. We are going to be wiped off the earth."

Mobile Bay

In August 1864, the Union enjoyed another important breakthrough that buoyed morale. The stranglehold on the southern ports was firm, but runners still penetrated the blockade at three principal ports. One of them was Mobile – the Confederacy's most important port in the Gulf. David Farragut, the daring conqueror of New Orleans, resolved to capture Mobile too, with a fleet of eighteen ships, including four ironclads.

On August 5, he led his ships toward the three forts in Mobile Bay. The Confederate guns started to roar against them. Undeterred by the savage bombardment, the 63-year-old admiral climbed the rigging and had himself lashed to it so that he could better survey the action over all the smoke and spray. The fleet braved the barrage and edged toward a string of mines (known then as torpedoes) which protected the mouth of the harbor. The leading

Farragut Entering Mobile Bay

ironclad, *Tecumseh*, hit one of them and went down, but Farragut remained firm. "Damn the torpedoes!" he bellowed, "Full speed ahead!" The fleet snaked through the minefield without loss while the rebel cannon raged overhead. Lurking beyond the minefield was the mighty Confederate ironclad, *Tennessee*, equipped with a formidable ram. But its puny engines gave it no chance of overpowering the Union fleet, which swarmed round her, hammering her with broadsides until she surrendered. Farragut then sealed off the bay to blockade runners and in the next few weeks, the rebel forts guarding it fell as well. The constricting grip of the Union blockade had tightened yet again, starving the South of much-needed supplies.

Who Will Lead the Union?

Northern morale had slumped during the summer of 1864, mostly due to hopes of a quick end to the war after Gettysburg and Grant's appointment being dashed. So far his campaign had seemingly done little but rob thousands of families of their beloved sons; casualties had been enormous and the gains appeared to be negligible. The deadlock between Grant and Lee at Petersburg only added to the sense of frustration. Gloomy war songs, such as *When This Cruel War Is Over* and *Bear This Gently to My Mother*, seemed to voice the depression of both civilians at home and soldiers on the front.

For Lincoln, melancholy and war weariness were the two evils that threatened his re-election; they were oxygen to the flames of anti-war Democrat and Copperhead propaganda that raged across the North. Even the Republicans had started to believe that their candidate was lost. One commented, "Lincoln's re-election [is] an impossibility . . . The people are wild for peace."

Lincoln would be up against General McClellan, a man eaten up with resentment against the President for taking him off the command of the Army of the Potomac. McClellan was running on the Peace Democrats' platform to stop the war even if it meant the end of the Union – just what the South wanted. The Confederate Vice President called McClellan's nomination "the first ray of real light since the war began." The War Democrats had sided with Lincoln; indeed his running mate, Andrew Johnson, was one of them. Always an army man at heart, however,

McClellan never fully resolved himself to the Peace Democrat agenda and often mumbled about upholding the Union through military muscle. Nor could he, much to his nominators' chagrin, bring himself to denounce the northern war effort as futile and a failure.

Lincoln's opponents began to whip up the race issue too, denouncing the Republicans for trying to establish "the equality of black and white races." The propagandists spread stories about "squint-eyed yellow babies" that had been born in New Orleans since its occupation by Union "abolitionists" who favored "miscegenation," "the blending of the white and black." The Emancipation Proclamation also came under attack not just from the Peace Democrats but from his own party, but Lincoln stayed firm, reiterating that his object was to restore the Union which could not be done "without using the Emancipation lever." Anyway, he had given his word to the freed slaves: "Why should they give their lives for us, with full notice of our purpose to betray them? . . . I should be damned in time and in eternity for so doing. The world shall know that I will keep my faith to friends and enemies, come what will."

Despite all the speeches, politicking and

disinformation, it was clear what mattered most in this election campaign – the predicament of the war itself. If the war effort was deemed to be a tragic waste of life that was going nowhere, the Democrats would sweep the board. On the flip side, if it looked as though victory was within the Union's grasp, then the man who had led the country to that great success must surely win. With only a few weeks before the nation went to the polls and still no good reports from the battlefields, Lincoln himself doubted his chances.

Suddenly, news of Union victories came in from across the country – Farragut at Mobile Bay, Sheridan in the Valley, and Sherman's mighty performance at Atlanta. It could not have come at a better time for Lincoln. The public's confidence in Lincoln, if it had wavered, now strengthened as the prospect of overall victory looked ever more likely. Until the results came in, however, Lincoln was not confident of success. But as it turned out, the public sent a resounding message that Lincoln's government was on the right course. He won a popular majority of fifty-five percent (more than seventy-five percent of the Federal soldiers voted for him despite their continued admiration of "Little Mac"), and took all the states except Kentucky, Delaware and New Jersey. Not only that, the Republicans scored huge gains in state legislatures and Congress, where they increased their majority to three-fourths. As much as showing its belief in Lincoln, the election explicitly demonstrated how much the North wanted to see the war through to its victorious end.

Chapter Seven

The Defeat of the South

With malice toward none; with charity for all; with firmness in the right, let us strive on to finish the work we are in; to bind up the nation's wounds; to care for him who shall have borne the battle, and for his widow, and his orphan – to do all which may achieve and cherish a just, and a lasting peace, among ourselves, and with all nations.

Abraham Lincoln

Making Georgia Howl

Having captured Atlanta to worldwide acclaim, William Tecumseh Sherman wanted to top even this victory with another dazzling campaign – to march his army across Georgia to the sea, tearing the Confederacy asunder, and destroying everything in his path. Sherman considered his force unstoppable and was sure he would "make Georgia howl." Lincoln and Grant were not so convinced. Sherman would be deep inside enemy territory, with his supply lines and all communication cut and with no prospect of reinforcement. But the vigor of his vision persuaded them, and on November 16, 1864, he began the march south-east.

Hood responded to this by heading in the opposite direction. He intended to bear down on Tennessee, knock out the Union communications with Sherman and strike the Ohio River, forcing Sherman to abandon his campaign and protect his rear. But Sherman was not to be distracted from his task. "If he will go to the Ohio River I'll give him rations," he said gleefully. "My business is down south." His army surged on toward Savannah on the coast, an irrepressible and virtually unopposed wave of blue that ravaged and

Union Troops Making Merry

wrecked everything it came across. The troops looted houses, stole food and burnt rebel supplies "like Demons." It turned out that the Georgia countryside had an abundance of supplies for Sherman's 62,000-strong army. And what they did not eat, they destroyed. The Union hell-raisers were having a ball, as one Yankee soldier confirmed: "This is probably the most gigantic pleasure excursion ever planned."

By mid-December, the Federals had reached Savannah. The city's 10,000 defenders thought better of facing the Yankee horde, and slipped away. Sherman sent word to Lincoln: "I beg to present you, as a Christmas gift, the city of Savannah, with 150 heavy guns and about 25,000 bales of cotton." The President was overjoyed, particularly in light of what had just happened in Tennessee.

Nashville

General John Bell Hood's boundless ambition was matched only by his military ineptitude. With 40,000 men – who were by now surviving on half rations and wearing tattered uniforms and shredded shoes – he intended to invade Tennessee and Kentucky, where he would recruit a further 20,000 sympathizers, destroy the 60,000-strong Union army under General Thomas (the Rock of Chickamauga), march to Virginia, reinforce Lee and conquer Grant and Sherman. Even by Hood's ambitious standards this was indeed a tall order.

At Spring Hill, Tennessee, Hood attempted to outmaneuver the Federal army, but a lack of coordination in the assault allowed the bluecoats to escape. In hot pursuit, the rebels caught up with the enemy at Franklin, fifteen miles short of Nashville. On November 30, Hood gave the command for a series of massive frontal assaults on the entrenched Union position. The ferocity of the rebel charges shattered the enemy line, but after furious hand-to-hand combat, the blues patched up the hole. The fighting went on into the night, until the Federals disengaged and withdrew to Nashville. Hood's victory at Franklin was surely a hollow one. He held the field but at the expense of more than 6000 of his precious men – three times that of the Federals – including dozens of his generals and officers.

Hood pushed on to Nashville regardless, laying a limp siege against the city with his outnumbered and demoralized force. Despite persistent orders from Grant, Thomas hesitated to attack, not realizing quite how battered his enemy was. On December 15 though, he was finally ready. Feinting on Hood's right, Thomas hurled the weight of his troops at the other side, demolishing the confused rebels. Toward nightfall, Hood's shattered army withdrew a couple of miles only to be set upon again the following day. In the driving rain, the overwhelmed Confederate line suddenly fell apart. Thousands turned and fled in panic, flinging their weapons away to speed their retreat, while thousands of others surrendered on the spot. It had been a disastrous rout and the once mighty Army of Tennessee was utterly defeated. What little remained of it was assigned to other forces and Hood, completely heartbroken, gave up his command.

Wilmington

The northern successes at the close of 1864 only increased southern woes at the beginning of 1865. Supplies of food, equipment, arms, ammunition and men were all running dangerously low. The Confederate dollar was plummeting in value, sinking to less than two percent of its original value. The Treasury was bankrupt, there were no troops left to keep Sherman in check, and Lee's army had received its last meat ration. In stark contrast, the war had actually stimulated the northern economy; coal and iron productivity had shot up, railroads and canal networks were spreading, the shipping industry was flourishing, and the US Navy was now the largest in the world. Lincoln boasted that the Union's resources were "now more complete and abundant than ever" and that the army was larger than at the outset of the war. "We are gaining strength," the President told Congress in December 1864, "and may, if need be, maintain the contest indefinitely."

Yet the South still refused to buckle and fall. It still had Lee and the Army of Northern Virginia, and as long as they held up so, Jefferson Davis believed, would the Confederacy. At this stage, Lee was getting most of his supplies from the Carolinas — and now the Federals set about putting an end to that too.

Wilmington, North Carolina was the focus of most of the rebel blockade–running activity, its port being heavily guarded by the enormous Fort Fisher on the Cape Fear River. Constructed with a twenty-five-foot thick wall of earth, tough grasses and logs that soaked up anything fired at it, the mile-long fort had plenty of powerful guns to menace any enemy ship that came close.

There had already been one attempt on the fort at the close of 1864, involving an impressive sixty-strong fleet under David Dixon Porter, supported on the land by Benjamin Butler's infantry units. Butler's idea of sending a ship crammed with explosives up to the fort was a miserable failure as was his subsequent land assault. In January 1865, Butler was replaced

General Benjamin F. Butler

by the keen and youthful General Alfred Terry, and another attempt was made. This time Porter's 600 navy guns pounded the fort's artillery into silence, and Terry's ground forces stormed the fort and waged a gritty battle with its defenders, soon overpowering the rebels. The loss of Fort Fisher, severed Wilmington's links with the sea, and cut a vital supply line to Lee's army. By February, hundreds of deserters were abandoning the Army of Northern Virginia every day. Many went to look after their starving families, others went looking for food and shelter for themselves, still more left because they believed the war was lost.

Into the Carolinas

Leaving a broad wake of devastation behind him on the way to Savannah, William T. Sherman decided that he should now turn his attention on the Carolinas as well. He and his troops felt they had a score to settle with South Carolina in particular – they were the ones that first seceded and started the war, after all. The whole army prickled with revenge and readied itself to lay waste to the land even more savagely than it had done in

Georgia. "I almost tremble at her fate," Sherman said, "but feel that she deserves all that seems to be in store for her."

Sure enough, Sherman's 60,000 bluecoats surged northward in February 1865, destroying and pillaging everything they came across, razing buildings to the ground, and setting houses to the torch. The lust to destroy was not even dampened by the wettest winter for twenty years, which turned roads to rivers that the Yankees waded through up to their armpits. Confederate engineers thought the state impassable, but Sherman pushed steadily forward, building bridges over swamps and rivers as quickly as he demolished the countryside.

In little more than a fortnight, the army had reached Columbia, the state capital, which was promptly converted into a smoldering pile of rubble. The South deplored the atrocity – and to this day the debate rages over who was responsible. Sherman denied he ordered it, and indeed there is some evidence that retreating rebel cavalry set fire to cotton bales in the streets before the bluecoats arrived. Either way, the resolute Sherman claimed not to have "shed any tears over the event." His troops cut the railroad link to Charleston, which soon fell, along with Fort Sumter. It was a

Charleston in Ruins

demoralizing and symbolic loss for the South.

In March, Sherman reached North Carolina, where his soldiers were considerably better behaved. He was aiming for Goldsboro where he was to join forces with 30,000 men from the coast, and march on to Petersburg. Joseph Johnston had the unenviable task of trying to stop him. Outnumbered three to one, Johnston launched a handful of attacks, delaying actions and ambushes, but was beaten back. Sherman, reinforced and supplied, pressed on to Virginia to help Grant win the war.

The Thirteenth Amendment

The Confederacy was fast running out of options. Only a year earlier it would have been as good as treason to suggest slaves be armed and sent to the front to fight alongside their white masters. Was the Emancipation Proclamation not "the most execrable measure recorded in the history of guilty man," according to Jefferson Davis? And yet now the South had very few alternatives.

Debate on the issue raged in the Confederate Congress and many still saw the idea as running against everything that the South was fighting for. Others saw it as the only way to keep slavery: "If emancipation of a part is the means of saving the rest, then this partial emancipation is eminently a pro-slavery measure." In the end, it fell on Lee to decide the matter and he was clear. Arming slaves was "not only expedient but necessary." "We should employ them without delay," he said. As it turned out, only Virginia state legislature actually passed the bill allowing for recruitment of slaves, and by the time black regiments were formed it was too little too late.

On a related measure, Confederates were sent to Europe, hoping to gain their recognition in return for abolishing slavery. Again, the idea would have been unthinkable a few years earlier, when, ironically, it was more than likely that London and Paris might have agreed. But now, in the desperate state the

Confederacy found itself, the proposition fell on deaf ears.

Meanwhile, in the North, events were unfolding that would also have been unimaginable a few years previously. Lincoln was pressing for a new amendment to the Constitution, its thirteenth, which would abolish slavery for good. Lincoln worried that the force of the Emancipation Proclamation would be severely weakened at the end of the war. Before the 1864 election, he had urged his party to include such an amendment as "the key stone" of his election platform. He took his ringing success at the polls as a strong endorsement of this from the people and immediately set about pushing it through Congress. Many Democrats were opposed to it, thinking it "unwise, impolitic, cruel, and unworthy of the support of civilized people." But Lincoln's aides secured enough support from them with promises of government jobs and favors in return for helping to steer the amendment through. On January 31, 1865, the Thirteenth Amendment was passed – with only a couple of votes to spare.

The result was met with rapture, cheers, and joyful weeping both in and outside the House. All recognized that it was a groundbreaking moment in the history of the nation. The next day, a black Massachusetts lawyer, John Rock, was admitted to practice before the Supreme Court by Chief Justice Salmon P. Chase. Only six years before, Chase's predecessor, Roger Taney, had ruled that black people were not even citizens. The Thirteenth Amendment enshrined in the Constitution the natural freedom of all, and set in motion the process which over the years would strive to achieve the civil and political equality for all.

One Last Hope

The winter of 1864–65 was one of the coldest Lee's soldiers could remember. His besieged army huddled together for warmth. Their torn and threadbare clothes, in the words of Sidney Lanier, a southern poet and soldier, "afforded no protection to anything but the insects congregated in the seams." Food rations were down to the barest minimum and soldiers began to fall prey to scurvy and pneumonia. By far the most infectious "sickness" of all, though, was homesickness. Families implored their sons to come home, and slowly Lee's great army had dwindled to only 30,000 as soldiers downed their guns and deserted. On the other side of the trenches, Grant's army was steadily gaining in numbers. Slowly, he extended his lines either side of the rebels, forcing Lee to do the same and spread his scant forces thinner still.

As Lee saw it, the Confederacy had one last hope. The Army of Northern Virginia must somehow slip out of Petersburg, unite with Johnston's forces and thrash Sherman before he reached Virginia. Then the combined rebel army could march back to Virginia and meet Grant on a more level footing.

On March 25, 1865, Lee made his move. In a surprise nighttime attack, the graycoats overran Fort Stedman east of Petersburg, capturing its batteries and half-a-mile of adjoining trenches. But before long the Federals had reorganized themselves and launched a crushing counterattack, which not only reversed all the rebel gains but smashed beyond them into the Confederate lines. Grant now seized the initiative and did not let go.

He sent Sheridan and his 12,000 cavalrymen, now returned from the Shenandoah Valley, to a crossroads known as Five Forks, which Lee would have to pass to get south to Johnston. Using rapid-

Union Cavalry

firing carbines, Sheridan's men gushed forward in closely coordinated attack, overwhelming the rebels sent there to defend it. Thousands were taken prisoner, thousands more fled for their lives in panic. When Grant heard the news, he knew the time was right for an all-out assault on the Confederate trenches. He had learnt the folly of frontal attacks on well-fortified positions, but the rebel line was now so sparse, Grant felt sure he could demolish it.

Just before dawn on April 2, the soldiers of the Army of the Potomac leapt out of their trenches, full of all the zeal of men who could taste victory. They burst irresistibly forward and pounded into the rebel lines. Lee's exhausted soldiers, ill-equipped and hungry, put up brave resistance and then withdrew westward, leaving Petersburg and Richmond to the Yankees. The weeping inhabitants of the Confederate capital packed up their possessions and fled by any means available; Jefferson Davis and his government boarded a special train for Danville. As the Union troops poured in, the Stars and Stripes was hoisted over the capitol to the horror of locals still there to see it: "We covered our faces and cried aloud. All through the house was the sound of sobbing. It was as the house of mourning."

The next day, Abraham Lincoln himself strode into the defeated rebel capital. It just so happened that he was visiting the Petersburg front when the fighting broke out, and had stayed on to witness the outcome. "Thank God I have lived to see this," he said. "It seems to me that I have been dreaming a horrid dream for four years, and now the nightmare is gone." As he walked through the rubble-strewn streets, black residents swarmed around him, the man who had won them freedom. "Glory to God! Bless the Lord! Glory, Hallelujah!" they cried, many of them on their knees before him in reverence. "Don't kneel to me. That is not right," Lincoln said. "You must kneel to God only, and thank Him for the liberty you will enjoy hereafter." The President strolled up to the capitol and when he sat down at Jefferson Davis's desk, a great roar went up from his soldiers outside.

The Final Chase

Lee's despondent and splintered army regrouped at Amelia Court House, some thirty-five miles west of Richmond. Here he expected to find vital rations to feed his starving men, and then turn south and rendezvous with Joseph Johnston's army in North Carolina. To his horror, all he found there were ammunition supplies – someone had made a mistake with his instructions. His men wasted a crucial day foraging the fields for food and begging at the little homesteads nearby, but there was virtually nothing to eat.

All the while, Sheridan's cavalry, like hounds on the scent of a kill, and over 100,000 Federals tore through the countryside in chase, making occasional thrusts at the straggling rebel soldiers, and preventing Lee from turning west. Many Confederates gave up, famished and exhausted, and simply sat down waiting to be captured. Others, surviving on horse-feed, kept up with their beloved general. One onlooker said about Lee himself, "He rode erect, as if incapable of fatigue . . . From his manner no man would have discovered that which he so well knew, that his army was melting away, that his resources were exhausted."

Desperate Rebel Resistance

At Sayler's Creek on April 6, the Federals hit the rear of Lee's scattered army, which fought a savage and desperate resistance. One eyewitness recalled, "I saw numbers of men kill each other with bayonets and the butts of muskets and even bite each other's throats and ears and noses, rolling on the ground like wild beasts." Even so, the rebels were hopelessly outnumbered and thousands were taken prisoner. "My God!" cried Lee when he saw it. "Has the army been dissolved?"

Two days later, Lee found himself surrounded. Sheridan's troopers had outrun him and cut off his passage west, his flanks were shut off and an immense sea of bluecoat infantry bore down on his rear. He resolved to make one last attempt to break out at dawn on April 9, a Palm Sunday. Lee's disheveled men fought bravely and pushed Union cavalry back –

but beyond them lay the vast expanse of Grant's forces. It would be hopeless to continue. "There is nothing left for me to do," Lee said, "but go and see General Grant, and I would rather die a thousand deaths."

Surrender

Lee sent a cavalryman galloping through Federal lines, a white towel tied his staff. Stunned Union soldiers stood in a bewildered silence. Could this really be an end to the war, an end to the pain, bloodshed, and suffering? Had they really won? An officer proposed three cheers, but there was only a

McLean's House at Appomattox Court House

limp reply from the soldiers' choked throats. Many of them just broke down and wept.

Lee and Grant agreed to meet at the nearby Appomattox Court House. It was owned by Wilmer McLean, who had moved from Manassas Junction after the battle there four years earlier hoping "never to see another soldier." Now the two great generals of the Civil War were agreeing terms of surrender in his living room. "The war began in my front yard," he joked, "and ended in my front parlor."

Grant's terms of surrender were magnanimous and fair. The soldiers would be paroled and not imprisoned nor tried for treason, officers would be allowed to keep their personal possessions, and men who had their own horses would keep them too. The generals signed, shook hands, and solemnly saluted

The Surrender at Appomattox

Lee Leaves Appomattox

each other. Grant sent food to Lee's men as a symbol of reconciliation, and prohibited his artillery from firing triumphal salutes. "The war is over," Grant told his men. "The rebels are our countrymen again, and the best sign of rejoicing after the victory will be to abstain from all demonstrations."

Lee mounted his horse and rode past his defeated men. The adoration they held for their general was as strong as ever, and they threw up cheers for him as he passed — wild cheers that soon turned to heartrending sobs. Lee raised his hat and turned to his men, his eyes brightly shining, and said, "I have done the best I could for you. Go home now, and if you make as good citizens as you have soldiers, you will do well, and I shall always be proud of you. Goodbye, and God bless you all."

A few other small Confederate armies still haunted the land, but when news of Lee's surrender reached them, they knew it was futile to continue the fight and laid down their arms. Jefferson Davis and his government fled into Georgia but were eventually captured by Union cavalry and imprisoned in Fort Munroe.

In the North, the public had barely recovered from the celebrations on the news of the fall of Richmond. Now they cheered, sang, and danced in the streets, hugging and kissing each other, while hundred-gun salutes went off in cities across the North. On April 11, Lincoln spoke to a joyful crowd from a White House balcony about his plans for the reconstruction of the new country. Lincoln wanted a nation at peace with itself, where no-one was victor or loser, a nation in which everyone – black and white – felt the future held promise for them and in which all would share the triumph of their common humanity. There would be no retribution or punishment, no trials for treason nor executions, and certainly no slavery. He believed both sides were to blame for the war and the terrible cost was in part God's retribution for the "offense" of slavery. He spoke of giving literate black men and black war veterans the right to vote.

But Lincoln was well aware that he could not move too fast if the public was not receptive to his generous and humane vision of a reconstructed America. As it turned out, Lincoln would not live to see his program implemented. For as he spoke there was one man in the crowd, an embittered actor, who certainly did not like what he heard. His name was John Wilkes Booth.

Assassination

A few days before the end of the war, Abraham Lincoln had a very disturbing dream. He told a friend about it: "There seemed to be a death-like stillness about me. Then I heard subdued sobs, as if a number of people were weeping. I thought I left my bed and wandered downstairs. There the silence was broken by the same pitiful sobbing, but the mourners were invisible. I went from room to room; no living person was in sight, but the same mournful sounds of distress met me as I passed along. It was light in all the rooms; every object was familiar to me; but where were all the people who were grieving as if their hearts would break? Determined to find the cause of a state of things so mysterious and so shocking, I kept on until I arrived at the East Room, which I entered. There I met with a sickening surprise. Before me was a catafalque, on which rested a corpse wrapped in funeral vestments. Around it were stationed soldiers who were acting as guards; and there was a throng of people. Some gazing mournfully upon the corpse, whose face was covered, others weeping pitifully. 'Who is dead in the White House?' I demanded of one of the soldiers. 'The President,' was his answer; 'he was killed by an assassin!' Then came a loud burst of grief from the crowd, which awoke me from my dream. I slept no more that night; and although it was only a dream, I have been strangely annoyed by it ever since."

On April 14, 1865, five days after Lee surrendered, Lincoln had no such morbid thoughts. It was Good Friday, a pleasant spring day, and the mood in Washington was still ecstatic. To celebrate the end of the war, he and his wife had arranged to see a comedy that night, *Our American Cousin*, at Ford's Theater. Little did they know that the actor, John Wilkes Booth, whom they had seen on stage a couple of years before, would also be making an appearance – though not in the play.

Booth was a racist, a white supremacist and a staunch believer in slavery. He also hated himself. He

Ford's Theater in Washington

considered himself a coward, too afraid to join the army to fight for his passionate beliefs. And the man he blamed for all his self-loathing and all country's "problems" was Abraham Lincoln. Booth had gathered a gang of slow-witted malcontents and with their help planned to kill not only Lincoln, but Grant, Vice-President Johnson and Secretary of State Seward too. An idiotic scheme to kidnap the President had come to naught a few months earlier, but now there was an opportunity to murder him that was too good to miss.

The audience was enjoying the show when Booth slipped into the President's box – Lincoln's guard had gone off for a drink. Booth drew a pistol, fired a round into the back of Lincoln's head, jumped out of the box snagging his foot on a flag, and landed on the

John Wilkes Booth Fleeing After Shooting Lincoln

stage in a heap. He stood up, shouted something and limped backstage to his horse on the street.

Lincoln was carried unconscious out of the theater across the street to a boardinghouse and put to bed. When a doctor saw the wound, he knew it was hopeless; the bullet was deeply embedded in his brain, lodged behind his eye. The next morning, surrounded by his weeping family and colleagues, Abraham Lincoln died.

The Nation Mourns

Lincoln's body lay in state in the East Room of the White House and then beneath the Capitol dome.

Abraham Lincoln

His casket was then transferred across the country by funeral train in a two-week journey of 1600 miles, passing all the major cities and towns on its way to Springfield, Illinois, where it was to be buried. Millions upon millions of mourners watched the parade or solemnly filed past the coffin, paying their last respects. The North was consumed with grief and many in the South, even so soon after the end of the war, were distraught at the loss. "Lincoln's death is one of the greatest misfortunes that could have befallen the country," wrote one southern planter. "From him we had a right to expect better terms of peace than from anyone else at all likely to come to power. Oh! My poor country. What have you yet to suffer?"

Before Lincoln's burial at Oak Ridge Cemetery, Springfield, the Union cavalry had caught up with his killer in Virginia. Booth resisted capture and was shot in the head. In June, eight people suspected to be in his gang were rounded up, hastily tried by a military commission and found guilty for their association with Booth and Lincoln's murder. Four were hanged, including a widow who kept a boardinghouse where they were supposed to have met.

It was almost six weeks after Lincoln's murder when the Stars and Stripes flew at full mast above the White House again. On May 23 and 24, 1865, the Grand Armies of the Republic marched in triumph from the Capitol down Pennsylvania Avenue – a procession of 150,000 soldiers in immaculate uniforms, their banners and standards fluttering in the light spring breeze. The new President, Andrew Johnson, and the man who would succeed him four years later, Ulysses S. Grant, were the chief dignitaries attending among a crowd of thousands. Spectators lined the route, singing, cheering and waving flags; children decked the soldiers with flowers and applauded these men and their dead comrades, heroes all.

The Wages of War

In the four years of the American Civil War, more than 620,000 soldiers were killed, around 360,000 of them Federals and 260,000 Confederates. No-one knows how many civilians lost their lives because of the war, but it is accepted as fact that more Americans died during those four years of war than in all America's other conflicts put together. Billions of dollars were wasted, new railroads demolished, towns razed to the ground, harvests burnt, livestock slaughtered, houses looted, lives ruined. When the war began, no-one knew that it would be so long and destructive. And when the ashes finally settled, many wondered whether it had all been worth it.

At the time, few northerners and black people could have doubted it. The Union had been preserved and four million slaves had won their freedom. And within a generation, once the wounds had healed, once distrust was replaced with confidence, once enmity had turned to friendship, few southerners doubted it either.

The Civil War not only finished the old southern way of life forever; it transformed the North too. All of American society was changed irreversibly by the war. At the end of the war, people felt that they were living in a new country, certainly one different from the one in which they were born. In those early years of peace, it was by no means a perfect country, and Lincoln's assassination only complicated an already delicate process of reconstruction.

But over time, it became clear that the war had created a nation dedicated to the great ideals embodied in Lincoln's address at Gettysburg – ideals of liberty and democracy that Americans have held sacred ever since. As Lincoln prayed at Gettysburg, the Civil War dead did not die in vain. Summing up the mood of the new United States, a rebel soldier wrote shortly after the war: "America has no north, no south, no east, no west. The sun rises over the hills and sets over the mountains, the compass just points up and down, and we can laugh now at the absurd notion of there being a north and a south. We are one and undivided."

Acknowledgments and Further Reading

With tens of thousands of titles in circulation, the American Civil War is one of the most written-about conflicts in world history. The following books, which were the principal sources for the quotations in this work, are recommended reading for anyone interested in finding out more about this fascinating subject.

Bruce Catton, *The American Heritage New History of the Civil War*, Viking, 1996.

Henry Steele Commager, *Illustrated History of the American Civil War*, Orbis Publishing, 1976.

William C. Davis, *The Battlefields of the Civil War*, University of Oklahoma Press, 1996.

James M. McPherson, *Battle Cry of Freedom: The Civil War Era*, Oxford University Press, 1988.

Geoffrey C. Ward, *The Civil War: An Illustrated History*, Knopf, 1990.